Fintech

Hacking, Blockchain, Big Data, Cryptocurrency (Financial Technology, Smart Contracts, Digital Banking, Internet Technology)

Eliot P. Reznor

Fintech: Hacking, Blockchain, Big Data, Cryptocurrency (Financial Technology, Smart Contracts, Digital Banking, Internet Technology)

Table of Contents

Book 1 - Hacking

Ultimate Hacking Guide For Beginners (Learn How to Hack and Basic Security through Step-by-Step Instructions)

1 - Introduction

I want to thank you and congratulate you for downloading the book Hacking: Ultimate Hacking Guide for Beginners. This book will give you the steps that you need in order to not only protect yourself from hackers but to be able to get into someone's computer system and access any files that they are saving on them.

Here is an inescapable fact: when you know the basics of hacking, then you are going to be able to look at your own security system on your network and know where you are need to add some extra security so that another hacker not able to get into your system. You can also use your new found skills to help your family members make sure that their computers and other devices are secure.

It is time for you to learn the basics of hacking so that you can practice and help advance your skills. Please note: this book is strictly for education purposes. This book will give you the steps needed to hack into individual objects.

The steps provided in this book should not be used in order to hack into something to do harm to another. Hacking is highly illegal, and you should never hack into a system without the administrator's permission.

Any hacking that is done without the expressed authorization of the system's administrator's permission is strictly illegal, and while you may not get caught right away, you can end up spending time in prison or paying some hefty fines. Any illegal hacking can earn you a sentence of up to twenty years in a federal prison.

2 - What is Hacking?

Technology is all around us. Everywhere that you look, someone, either has a phone or a tablet in their hands. Our entire lives revolve around technology. But, what most people do not realize is that even that phone or table that you are toting around everywhere is can be hacked.

Hacking is known as the act of getting into a computer and modifying the software and hardware to accomplish a goal that is outside of the administrator's original purpose for the machine. People who perform these acts are called hackers.

A hacker exposes the weakness of the security in a computer so that they can gain access to the computer's system. Hacking can be used to obtain access to someone's personal information and sell it or to protest a point. However, there are people who use hacking just because they enjoy the challenge or because they are working for a company or the government to help them add extra security to their system.

Hacking is the opportunity to demonstrate one's skills not just to harm others. Computer hacking is used for real life application of problem-solving skills that you most likely learned in school. A hacker typically enjoys programming and has expert skills in their particular programming area.

Much to people's surprise, hackers are usually self-taught and are employed by major companies as part of their IT staff. Using their unique set of skills, they find the flaws that are in the security of the business's system so that the holes can be repaired quickly.

This helps a lot of companies avoid people breaking in and stealing sensitive information about the company that can be used in order to harm the company or its employees. A lot of hackers have been known to help with technological developments thanks to their programming skills. Napster was created by a hacker believe it or not.

Ultimately hackers are just people who want to satisfy their intellectual curiosity. But, just like other skills, people are going to use their hacking skills in order to cause harm and gain access to personal and financial information.

To safeguard yourself from hackers, you need to have a firewall in place. Also, make sure that you keep your security system and computer software is up to date on the most current version so that you can protect yourself further.

3 - Hacking Methods

A hacker finds the security flaws in a system and exploits them for good or to get ahold of their sensitive data and end up destroying someone's life.

Ways to think like a hacker

Identify their exploits so that you can create a footprint analysis. This is you getting as much data as you possibly can on your hands on about your target. Think about the size of your target along with any potential entry points that you can utilize to get into their network. Think about the company's domain names, IP address, subsidiaries, and phone numbers.

Look at back door entry points. Startup companies may have a weak security system because it may not have the money in their budget to make sure that they are using a good security system. You will also find this problem in companies that have just been bought out by a larger company. In hacking into smaller companies, you might find information for larger companies that may become your next target.

Connect to the TCP and UDP ports. This is going to enable

you to send out random data to determine the web server, mail server, and File Transfer protocol that is your target is using.

Many UDP and TCP servers send back data that will allow you to identify applications that are running because of data that you sent out in the first place. Thanks to this, the weaknesses can be discovered by cross-referencing the data that you discovered in a vulnerable database like SecurityFocus.

In order to gain access to a network, you can use a username and a password. Having a username and a password is going to allow you to sneak into the system and set up an attack without them ever knowing because it will seem as if you belong there.

When you have gotten into the network, then can take the information that you gain from their website and call an employee directly. Tell them that you are from IT and trying to fix a problem with the system.

Many times the employee will know that you do not work for that company and they are going to provide you with any information that you are seeking. Be sure that you are authentic in what you are saying so that they do not suspect that you are an intruder.

Using the password and username that you have obtained, used it to get into the company much like the Greeks did with the Trojan Horse. You are will want to replace software such as Notepad with a piece of Trojan code that will allow you to have access to the system at a later date.

You are also going to be automatically added to the administrator's group so that you have instant access to any information that is "admin only."

Software and Hardware Keylogger

Keylogger is a program that allows you to have a record of every keystroke that is made by a computer. This makes it easier for a hacker to get a hold of passwords and any other sensitive information on a computer without the user ever knowing that it is happening.

Software keylogger

This software can easily be downloaded to a victim's computer so that it can begin to capture every keystroke that is made. The software can be set up to send a summer of all keystrokes in a file to an email so that it can be analyzed later. If you work from home, this is going to put all your work files at risks as well as any personal information.

CNET offers a free keylogger. If CNET does not do everything that you want, do a Google search for other software that you can download. Some of the ones that you have to pay a small fee for to may end up having all the features that you are wanting.

Hardware keylogger

Just like software keylogger only uses hardware instead. Files cannot be emailed because they are stored on a USB drive. The USB drive is put into the victim's computer to capture all of the keystrokes that they make.

Keelog offers a USB that has the program already installed on it but it is priced higher. If you do not want to buy a USB that already has the program on it, then you can download the program to your own USB for cheaper.

Stealing Cookies

Cookies allow a website to stockpile the information that you put into it. The information is then stored on a hard drive. Cookies contain valuable information for tracking a session. As long as the hacker is on the same Wi-Fi as the victim, they are going to have access to this information. Public WiFi's make this easier for a hacker

A hacker copies and clones the cookies so that they can deceive the website into believing that the cookies have been authenticated. Firesheep helps to sniff out web traffic on open Wi-Fi connections so that it can collect cookie and store them on the hacker's internet browser.

A hacker can click on cookies that are saved and have an entryway to the target's accounts that they are logged into. As soon as you log off, the hacker will no longer have access to any sensitive information.

Phishing

This is a more difficult hacking option, but it allows a hacker to gain access to your accounts. Hackers create a fake login page and then send it to your email. Being that the page looks exactly like the page that you are used to logging into, you are going to attempt to log into the page.

However, you are sending all of your login data to a person instead of the real website's servers. The hacker will have to establish a web hosting account along with the fake login page and ensure that the pages look real or else the victim is not going to fall for it.

After having created the page, make sure that details that may be noticed are tweaked before you submit the form, copy it, and store it, before emailing it out to the target. A way to avoid this is to be careful about logging into any pages that may not seem like the real deal.

Email security systems have gotten better at where these emails are usually filtered directly into the spam box. However, to bypass this, as a hacker, the entire page is going to have to be duplicated in order for the email filter to believe that you are the real deal. Email is the most commonly known phishing scam.

4 - Types of Hackers

There are different levels of hacking, and each hacker is going to fall into a different category. The groups are labeled as good, bad, and the in-between hackers.

White hat hackers

This is a term used for an ethical hacker or computer security expert. These hackers generally specialize in penetration testing along with the use of other methods to ensure the safety of an organization's security system. Ethical hacking was a term coined by IBM; it encompasses more than just those that use penetration testing.

White hat hackers do not hack for malicious intent. This term was coined from the Old West films where the heroes wore white hats. Other names for a white hat hacker are tiger teams, sneakers, or red teams. Hackers who do phreaking are known as white hat hackers. Well, known white hat hackers are Kevin Poulsen, Kevin Mitnick, and Eric Corley along with many others.

Black hat hackers

These hackers are known for violating a computer's security

system just to be malicious. Black hat hackers normally are the ones who take personal information and sell it for personal gain. The term was first used by Richard Staliman when speaking about a criminal hacker and how they differ from someone who hacks just for curiosity.

Black hat hackers are the general idea of what society thinks about hackers. These are the hackers are portrayed as the ones that are "the epitome of all that the public fears in computer crimes." This type of hacker will generally break into a secure network and modify, destroy, or steal data that is stored there.

They also have the ability to make the system unstable for anyone who is authorized to actually use it. Hackers that use cryptovirology are known as black hat hackers. The term black hat came from the Old West films much like the white hat name did, only this is because the antagonist usually wore a black hat.

Gray hat hackers

These hackers frequently fall somewhere in between the black hats and the white hats. They generally hack a computer system and sometimes violate the ethical standards and laws. They do not hack for malicious intent. This term was first brought around in the 90s so that hackers that were not a white hat or black hat would have a name.

Another way to tell the difference is to see the methods that they use to discover vulnerabilities. A gray hat hacker will charge a small fee to the company to find small weaknesses in their system so that they can fix the holes in the network.

When looking at an SEO community, a gray hat hacker is defined as someone who manipulates a web site's ranking on a search engine by using improper or unethical means that are not considered to be search engine spam.

5 - Hacking Pre-Requisites

Hacking is not a skill that people are born with. It must be learned over a set period of time so that you can become good at it. Whether you are aspiring to be a white hat hacker or a black hat hacker (although it is illegal to do the crimes that black hat hackers commit) you will want to go through a process to do what you are wanting achieve.

The primary thing that you are going to need to remember to become a hacker is that you need to have patience.

Steps to begin your hacking journey

Begin using the Kali Linux system on a daily basis. Learn data structure and algorithms on a deeper level. In a computer class, this is taught in the second year. But, you are also going to want to know how to use data structures and algorithms as they pertain to Python and the C programming languages.

Have an understanding of how operating systems work

Have a solid understanding of memory management as well as process management along with cryptography, IP/TCP, and routing protocols. Understand how websites work. You will need to learn JavaScript, HTML, and Apache. It is also helpful to know PHP, CSS, My SQL and Django.

Have a clear and concise understanding of vulnerabilities and possible attacks

Get familiar with hacking tools such as SQL map, Wapiti, Cain and Abel and Aircracking. After some practice with the tools, make your own tool that is unique to what you want to do. Do not get in a hurry. Learning to hack is not like learning to read or ride a bike. Using someone else's tools does not make you a hacker.

Talk to someone who has been in hacking for a while and gets some advice on how you should proceed. Be a good guy, not a bad guy. When you are hacking, do not use your skills to harm someone else. Use them to help others. Find a guy in a Fortune Five Hundred company and help expose their weaknesses.

6 - Step by Step Guide to Hacking

Hacking used to be used to help gain information about a system for IT purposes until it was brought to the public's eye as something that was bad. Thanks to that, hacking has taken a darker turn causing people to fear those who do hacking, even if they do not do it with any malicious intent.

Before you begin

Programming is a necessity when you are planning on hacking. There are various programming languages that you can learn, but you should try and learn all of them so that you are well rounded and know how each program speaks while working with the operating system. The more you know, the easier it is going to be for you to gain access to networks.

Know all that you can possibly know about your target. Getting this information is going to help you expose their weak spots and therefore make it almost effortless for you to get into their system. Look at different approaches in case your initial plan does not go the way that you planned.

The more knowledge that you have on your target, the less chance you are going to find surprises when you get into hacking their system. When gathering information, you are doing what is known as enumeration.

Hacking

Use a nix screen for all your commands. Cygwin and Nmap are two programs that will help you when it comes to the nix terminal. Ensure that the machine you are using to hack is secured. If you are not secured, then you leaving yourself open to being found out. If someone traces you then they can file a lawsuit against you because they are now going to know exactly who you are.

If you do not feel comfortable hacking into someone else's system, even if you have obtained permission, then you can hack into your own system to find your own security flaws. In order to hack your own system, you are going to need to set up a virtual laboratory.

Make sure that you can reach the system that you are trying to hack; this basically means make sure that the computer is on. When using a ping utility tool, you are going to need to test and see if your target is active, just remember that the results cannot always be trusted. The biggest flaw with a ping tool is that the system administrator can turn their system off, therefore, causing you to lose your target.

Run a scan of all the ports that you are going to be attempting to attack by using pOf or Nmap. This is going to tell you if the ports are active or not which means that they are going to be open for you to access.

Ports that use HTTP or FT are going to be less protected and once hacked; they will be unsecure and discoverable. Passwords can be cracked by using brute force. By using brute force, you will try every possible combination that is listed within a pre-determined list.

Algorithms are going to improve your cracking speed. The hashing of algorithms can be weak therefore are exploited by using their weakness to gain access to the system.

Graphics cards can be used as another processor of sorts. Gaining access through a graphics card is going to be a thousand times faster than it will be for you to crack a password or algorithm. Do not attempt to use every possible password or you are going to get locked out because you have polluted the system and it can take years to actually complete this process.

When using an IP address, you are going to need to have a rooted tablet and the TCP program installed. TCP is going to upload and allow you to gain access to any site that is secured.

If you are targeting a nix machine, you will need to have root privileges. So that you can see all of the files that are on the system, you will be required to have super user privileges. When you have super user privileges, you will be allowed to have an account so that you have access to everything as a root user in the system.

You can create a buffer overflow so that you can give yourself the super user status. The buffer overflow is going to allow a memory dump therefore giving you access to inject a code so that you can perform a task that is at a higher level than what you are authorized to do.

Now you have worked so hard at getting in the system; you do not want to take up too much time getting out of the system. The moment that you have access to a system that uses an SSH server, you are going to want to create what is known as a backdoor so that you can regain access to the system when you want to get back in it.

It is of vital importance that you do not allow the system administrator to know that you were in their system or that it may be compromised. Do not make any changes to the website or create any more files than what you need to. Do not create additional users or you'll send up red flags to the administrator.

7 - Techniques That Are Used by Hackers

Techniques can be used in everything. With hacking, techniques can help you with getting in and out of a network undetected as well as give you several methods just in case your first one does not work out while you are in the middle of trying to hack a system.

Anonymity: Hackers do not want anyone knowing that they have hacked into their system. When a hacker worms their way into a system, they are able to do it without a trace. However, in order to do this, they use:

- Secure tunnels

- Proxies

- Software that helps to hide their IP address

- Other people's usernames and passwords

- Programming that is written in C

- Telenet that helps hide him and the tasks that he is executing.

Getting out

A good hacker is going to ensure that they do not leave a trace on the system that they were on. In the process of getting out, the hacker is going to leave all your files alone. But, they are keep a "backdoor" open so that he can get back into the computer at a later date.

Gathering information about the target: Before hacking someone, get as much information as possible on them. You are going to want information like:

- Telnet or Tracert to look at the pings of when someone is using the computer

- Their IP address

Be resourceful

Find out as much about your target as you can get. Even if you do not think that it is helpful, it may be useful in the long run.

Log the keystrokes

You are able to use programs that will review every keystroke that someone has made on their computer and that alone can result in revealing a person's identity.

Go for passwords

When trying to hack someone's password, it is best to try the simple algorithms that create a combination of letters, numbers, and symbols. This is a trial and error method. You are going to need to make well-educated guesses and use dictionary attacks so that you can generate every password combination possible.

Leave a virus

This leaves a way back into the computer. Leaving a virus can be done by sending an email or instant message to your victim.

Gain entry through the back door

This is similar to hacking a password. Many hackers develop codes and programs that find pathways that are left unsecured into a system. They never have to use a password this way.

Spy through email

This program can be utilized so that you can interrupt emails and read them.

Make zombie computers

When a computer is used by a hacker to place DDoS attacks and send out spam emails, it is called a zombie computer. If an innocent user clicks on the link that you sent out, then it will open up an instant connection between the host computer and his.

Ensure that you have a firewall up so that you are able to restrict access to any personal information that may go outside of your computer's system.

Use proxy servers

When you have decided which computer you are going to hack, make sure that you target the proxy servers.

Use search engines

Search engines can help to find the resources that are needed to hack a system. From there, you will be able to download the tools so that you can target the computer that you have chosen.

Leave a file or two

Leaving files will allow you to gain access to the computer whenever you want. You can leave files such as Net cat in order to gain access again. Just make remember that you should not leave too many or else the system administrator will notice.

8 - The Effects of Hacking

When you hack into a computer, you are opening up the system to multiple effects. As the public sees, many of the consequences of hacking are going to be bad because the public does not always see that hacking is sometimes a good thing.

When you hack someone, you are always leaving them open to the malicious effects of what hacking brings about whether you mean to or not. If you are going to hack into someone's system, you need to think about what you are going to be leaving them open to if you are not careful.

While you may be hacking them to show them where they have their security flaws, you are going to want to ensure that they close those holes so that they can protect themselves from other hackers who may not be as nice as you.

Effects of Hacking

When hacking into a computer, you create a breach in the security system. This places the victim's sensitive data and privacy at risk. Hacking activities are generally done to gain access to confidential information that one tends to keep on their network. Information like this can be social security numbers, credit card numbers, bank account data, personal photographs, etc.

Very few hackers take information to cause harm, in fact, many of them take it just to show that their target has major security issues that need to be fixed. After the security system has been compromised, there is a possibility of loss or even manipulation of data. A hacker can delete any sensitive information that has been placed on a network.

Once a system has been hacked, the victim is at risk of all their data being lost or manipulated. One of the biggest things that people associate with hackers is identity theft. Identify theft is when someone who is not authorized takes your identity. Your identity is not just conclusive to your date of birth and your social security number. It also includes anything that identifies you as you.

Someone taking your identity is usually done with malicious intent and used for the hacker's personal interest. After you have been hacked, a hacker can track everything that you do on your computer with the advances that there have been in technology. Keylogging is just one of the programs that hackers can use in order to track your keystrokes.

8 - THE EFFECTS OF HACKING

With this software, hackers are instantly able to grab all the information that they want from you. DOS means denial of service attack. A DOS attack is when a hacker gets into your network and makes your computer resources unavailable to any authorized users.

A DOS can be used to attack a website and make the site unavailable for an unknown period of time. Having a website down can be an inconvenience and hamper any business that is done on the site. Stolen information happens when someone hacks your network for malicious reasons.

This is hazardous to anyone and most particularly business' that are hacked. Sensitive information that is released from companies may be information that they do not want the public knowing yet. It also compromises employee contact details and client information.

National security can be put at risk due to hacking. Hackers who get into the government's networks have access to the defense system and various other systems. This can cause grave consequences on the welfare of the nation. When someone hacks into the government not only is the nation at risk, but the citizens of the United States are as well.

Another effect of hacking is fraud. Hackers are able to turn computers into zombies by infecting them with internet enabled computer viruses. These computers are then used for activities that are considered fraud. Fraud activities include but are not limited to spamming and phishing attacks that are done on other networks.

How do you know if your computer has been hacked?

- Your computer is most likely going to decrease in performance speed

- You are going to begin to notice files that are not supposed to be there

- Files may increase in size

- Files may be modified without you ever touching them.

- Network settings are changed

- You experience frequent disk crashes.

How to protect your computer

- Install a reliable antivirus software

- Make sure that your firewall is enabled before connecting to the internet

- Install system updates on a regular basis.

9 - Hacking into a Computer

To be able to hack into a computer is a rare and useful skill. You can get past a password if you have locked yourself out of your computer or are wanting to check up on a family member to see what they are doing.

You will be able to gain remote access to a computer in case your computer that has been stolen and you are trying to locate it. Then, to top it all off, you can hack into a Wi-Fi connection to look up directions in case you are lost in an unfamiliar city.

A lot of the steps that you are will use in order to hack into a computer were discussed in a previous chapter.

Hacking into a computer

A programming language is a necessity when you want to learn how to hack. The more you know about how a computer talks to the operating system, the easier it will for you to gain access to the network.

Know your target

Get as much information on your target as you can. The

more informed you are, the less likely you are to be caught off guard.

Hacking logins

Boot your computer up into safe mode. Click on the start menu and select the run option. Once the run command box has opened, type in "control userpasswords2." At this point in time, you are going to have the ability to change the password to any account that is on the computer.

This is going to be blatantly obvious to the user whose password that you changed. If you click the button two times, you are going to be able to put in recover password should you get locked out of the system and then you will be able to set up a new password so that you can log back in. The final step is to reboot your computer to make sure that the changes were saved.

Remote hacks

You are going to want to download the program LogMeIn. This program is free, and you can purchase it later to have everything that meets your hacking needs. This program is going to require download onto both computers. This will become helpful if your computer is stolen or you want to gain access to your child or spouse's computer.

You will need to have an account on the program's website to use the software. Log into the LogMeIn website. Go to the "my computers" tab which should open as soon as you have logged into the website. Add different computers that you are going to want to access remotely.

After all the computers have been added, you are going to be allowed to log into the computer. This means that you are going to need to have knowledge of the login information for the account that you are trying to hack.

You will now want to click on the remote control. If you want to remotely access it without anyone knowing that you are getting into it, then try not to move the mouse and do not click on anything or else they are going to see that you are spying on them. Log out, and no one is ever going to know that you were ever on their computer

Hacking Wi-Fi

Wireless networks are routers or any other way that a person can get Wi-Fi in their home or business. They can be easily hacked because a lot of people do not change the password to the router from the original password that was given by the wireless provider.

Be sure that you have the appropriate programs downloaded. Two programs that you can use are CommView and AirCrackNG. These programs are going to locate the vulnerabilities that are in the system so that you can help break the security code.

Find a network. CommView is going to scan for any wireless network that it can find. All you need to do is select a network that has a WEP key as well as a decent signal. Filter your search specifically to the network that you have chosen. Right click on which one you plan to use.

Select the copy MAC address. Go to the rules tab and down to the MAC addresses. You will enable the MAC address rule. Click action, capture, add record, both before you paste the MAC address. From here you are going to sort out the management and control files so that you are only seeing the data packets

By going to the logging tab, you can enable the auto saving

mode. You may be required to modify the settings on the directory size and file size. Try 2000 and 20. Press the play button so that you can begin collecting. You will have to wait until you have around 100,000 packets. At this point, you will click concatenate logs to make sure that all the logs are selected.

Transfer the logs out of the program. Find the folder where your logs are saved and select it. Click on the file and export it before selecting WireShark/TCP dump format. Save it so that you can locate it later. Open the file with AirCrack. Enter your index number. As soon as the command box appears, you will need to input the index number for the Wi-Fi network that you are targeting.

Once you have done this, you are going to hit enter and wait. If it works, then the passkey is going to be shown on your screen.

10 - How to Protect Your Computer

How do you protect your computer against attacks? Some of the ways have been previously touched on earlier. Protecting yourself is necessary to make sure that you are not losing valuable material that can harm you later.

Methods for protecting your computer

Make sure that you keep your files and folders backed up. Store them in a different location that is not your computer. There are places online where you can store stuff for free such as Dropbox and OneDrive. Have a good firewall in place.

A good firewall prevents spyware, Trojan viruses, and other viruses from infecting your computer. Some applications want you to disable your firewall, use your best judgment on if you should or not. Review all your browser and email settings for their security. Make sure that you constantly erase cookies on your computer

Cookies are not going to pose any threat to damaging computers, but they do track what you do online on a daily basis. Set your internet zone for high and your trusted sites for at least medium low. Disable any unnecessary JavaScript or ActiveX file content. Hackers are going to use ActiveX or JavaScript in order to plant a virus that can harm your system.

Install software that will capture any viruses and make sure that it is going to automatically update. New viruses are being discovered every day. Keep your program updated regularly so that any new viruses that come out can be caught by a properly updated antivirus program.

If you get a message from someone that you do not know personally and it contains an attachment, do not open it. This is an easy way for hackers to get viruses into your system. If something comes from someone that you do not know or comes from someone that you do know but are not expecting anything from, be safe and simply delete it.

Make sure that you only download from places that you trust. Do not send files from unknown sources to friends or family. This is a good way to viruses being sent out from your computer to theirs. Always turn off your computer and disconnect from the internet.

If your system is shut off and not even logged into your network, then hackers are not going to be able to gain access to your system thus keeping you protected. Never use the same one password. Use a two-step authentication. It will ask for a second password when your password has been entered incorrectly

Sites like LinkedIn or Twitter are going to give you a code to enter when you attempt to log into your account from a new device. If you change your phone number or email, make sure to update it with the site as well. Only use sites that have HTTPS.

When setting up your home Wi-Fi, set it up with a password. Most routers come with a sticker on the side of the box that will give you access to the network. Make sure that you change it. Do not stick with the default password because it is too easy to be hacked. Also, when a machine asks what kind of security encryption you want, you should choose WPA-2.

It is wise to attempt to avoid WEP and WPA at all costs. The encryptions actually have a flaw that will give up the password within a few seconds. Hide your router with an SSID.

With technology everywhere, we now have smart fridges, ovens, and washer and dryers.

Devices like this allow you to connect to the internet so that you have different options that original designs do not have. The companies that are putting out these highly advanced devices are still working out the kinks. The companies that are pushing these devices out with Wi-Fi connectivity forget important things like privacy and safety for their device's users.

An example of this is someone that hijacked a baby monitor and said foul mouthed things over the monitor. In the end, security over your devices is up to you so that you can protect yourself.

11 - Additional Ways to Protect Yourself from Hackers

Through the various chapters in this book ways to protect yourself have been talked about, but there are a few other ways that you can add some extra security to your system so that it is harder for hackers to gain access to your accounts.

The first thing you are going to want to remember is that nothing is unhackable. Hardware and software can be hacked by the right person who has enough skills and patience.

Methods to use to protect yourself

Password Managers

A password manager is going to help prevent someone from guessing your password or using brute force to crack it. Password generators will give you random passwords that you do not have to think of and that are going to be harder for a hacker to crack.

Applications like LastPass, RoboForm, and 1Password are applications that can cross platform.They will not work on your computer, but they will work on your phone quite well.

Two-factor authentication

This is a stop gap for when you are trying to log into a website that has not been used on that device before. The two-factor for Twitter will send you a text message with an alternate but temporary passwordThis will allow you to log into Twitter from that device without the password that you have set up because they are trying to ensure that it is you getting into your account.

You are alerted for when someone is attempting to get into your account. This even happens if they are using your set password, but are using a different device. Twitter, Apple, Google, Dropbox, and Microsoft are just a few sites that use two-factor authentication. Do not back up sensitive data on your phone or online.

Even though the cloud is supposed to be secure, it is not. Do not put videos, images, or documents on external servers. So do not use Dropbox or Flikr. Instead, use an external drive that you can access offline. This means that you should not put your phone data on the cloud. The cloud is a treasure trove of data to a hacker. Keep your backup protected and local.

Do not link accounts

Linking accounts give hacker to everything that they may not have had access to before. It is difficult to keep accounts separated nowadays because everything is now allowing you to log in through the use of another account that you have already created.

It is possible for you to keep the accounts separated, though. Use unique logins and passwords for everything that you do. Check and see what applications you have tied to Facebook and Twitter. If you are not using it, then remove it.

Security questions

Security questions were questions that are meant to keep your information safe. Now they are things that allow you to have a simple and easy access to your account. Do not answer the question with the truth, instead use a unique answer that makes no sense to the question. For example,

"What is your favorite color?" Answer: "Snoop Dogg." Make sure that you can remember the answer.

Misinformation

You are already answering your security questions, with a lie, why not continue for the sake of online security. The most powerful tool you will have is misinformation. Change the key to all things that use security questions. This includes information such as your birthday, family ties, birthplace, and billing address.

If you are friends with your family on social media, do not let anyone know it is your family. People can easily figure out your mother's maiden name if they know who is on your friend's list.

Password protect all your devices

This should be top priority when you get a new device. Any computing device is simply a giant bag that contains all of your personal information. If it was to get stolen, then you would be making it easier for your hacker to steal your identity if you do not password protect it.

You are not only saving yourself but your contacts as well. When getting into a person's account the first thing a hacker is going to go after is their contacts for their emails

Site-specific credit card numbers

Many banks are able to give you a temporary card number. They may even be able to give you a one-time use card number. Any kind of credit card number is easily tied to you, and therefore your information can be taken.

All a hacker needs is the last four of your card number to hack your identity.If you are using different cards that are all linked to the same bank account, then when one card is compromised, all of them will be.

Privatize your website

If you happen to own a domain name, there are chances that some of your private information is easily accessible to anyone who does a whois query. You can hide your domain registration in order to protect yourself. Sign into your domain

Look for the option that allows you to privatize your information. Should you not find this option, you need to call the site's support and have them walk you through how to do it. It may cost you a small fee each year, but it is worth it.

12 - A Hacker's Mindset

There are five main principals that a hacker should think about when they are hacking.

The principals of hacking

The world is full of intriguing problems that are just waiting to be solved. As a hacker, you can have a lot of fun as long as you are doing it legally. It takes a lot of effort to be a hacker, and it also takes a lot of motivation. As a hacker your motivation is going to come from you solving problems, exercising your intelligence and sharpening your skills with each successful hack.

You were not born with hacking skills; you had to learn the ways of being a hacker. You are able to learn how to hack anything you need to. If you are able to tackle a problem and learn how to solve one piece at a time. You will have learned something and are ready to learn the next thing. Have faith in yourself and your ability to learn how to solve a puzzle one piece at a time.

No problem needs to be solved twice. Your creative brain is both a valuable and limited resource. Do not waste time on re-inventing the wheel. If a problem has been solved, move onto a different problem that has not been solved before. In order to act like a hacker, you need to believe that your time is precious.

Thinking that it is your moral duty to share any information that you have from solving problems as well as solving any problem before you just give the solution away.

This will help other hackers to be able to work out new problems that arise instead of having to solve ones that you may have answers to. Just because a problem has been solved, does not deem that you should not go back and try to find another solution that might make solving it easier. There is never just one solution to any given problem.

Often times we learn a lot from the problems that we did not know before by examining the first solution to the problem. It is okay for you to believe that you can do better than the person that came up with the first solution. It is not alright for you to use technical, legal, or even institutional barriers in order to prevent a solid solution from being reused therefore causing others to reinvent the wheel.

You do not need to feel obligated to hand over your creative product. You may want to remember that hackers are the ones that will give you the most respect as a hacker. It is perfectly okay for you to use your hacking skills in order to support your family or get rich.

Do not forget where your loyalties are to the art form of hacking. And do not forget your fellow hackers who are the people who helped you on your way up. Boredom and routine work are evil. Being that hackers are naturally creative, you should never get bored or have to drudge at work that is repetitive

This will cause you to not be able to solve new problems which are the whole reason why you are doing what you do. Boredom and drudgery are not just undesirable, but actually evil to a hacker. In order to behave like a hacker, you are going to need to believe this enough to ensure that you do not fall into boredom.

You also need to have the realization of when you have hit a wall so that you can come up with a solution to get yourself off of it. You need to do this not only for yourself but others as well. Just like most important things, there is an expectation of this rule. As a hacker, you are going to do things that are repetitive or even boring to a normal observer

These are done as mind clearing exercises. Or they can be used to acquire a skill that you have no experience in. You can also sharpen your skill in a certain area. This type of boredom is okay because it is by choice. You should never allow yourself to be forced into a situation that is going to cause you to be bored and stifle your creativity.

Freedom is good

As a hacker, you are most likely anti-authoritarian. This does not mean that you lack any respect for authority, but some hackers allow it to go that far. When someone gives you an order that will stop you from solving a problem you are fascinated by, it will generally cause you to work at an accelerated rate to solve the problem.

As most authority minds think, they will find some sort of reason as to why it is stupid that you are attempting to solve the problem. Therefore, it is important you try and fight this type of mindset. This does not require that you are fighting all authority. As a hacker, you are going to need to accept some sort of authority so that you are able to get things that you want.

This does not mean that you are required to allow the authority to smother you and stop you from hacking. To behave like a hacker, you should develop a natural hostility to any:

- Censorship

- Use of force

- Deception

Censorship is used to blind adults that are responsible. You will need to act on that single belief alone. Attitude is not a substitute for competence. If you are a hacker, then you are naturally going to have some attitude.

Copping an attitude alone will not going to make you a hacker. To be a hacker, it takes practice, dedication, hard work, and intelligence. Because of this, you need to learn to distrust any attitude given to you and respect the competence of every kind

Hackers are not going to let some hacker waste their time.

But they will worship competence. Especially when that competence is with hacking, but proficiency at anything should be valued. Competence is demanding skills that very few can master which is good. Competence at demanding skills that involve mental craft, concentration, and acuteness is even better.

If you are able to reverse competence, you will then enjoy developing it in your own work. Hard work and dedication will bring about intense play rather than drudgery. This attitude is vital to you starting your journey as a hacker.

13 - Pursuing a Career in Ethical Hacking

Not all hackers are going to be hacking into a system in order to gain an entry way to your personal information. Several very famous hackers have come out of history and given us the technology that we enjoy in our everyday lives. these men are Steve Jobs, Steve Wozniak, and Captain Crunch.

Starting your career

It is wise that you have a computer science degree. Many big companies hire hackers to find flaws in their systems so that they are able to keep their company secrets, secret. You can use hacking skills to make your own technology. You will be able to create programs and computers to help protect people from hackers.

If you want to go to a company and work for them, find the companies that are hiring people for their IT teams. You will be doing more than just finding security flaws in their system. Remember that hacking is illegal unless it is done ethically.

Punishments if caught hacking illegally

India

If you are found tampering with a computer source document by using destruction or concealment methods. Or even altering the documents source code, you can get three years in prison and a fine of 20000 rupees. If you are found having hacked into a website or other sources, you can be imprisoned for three years or fined 50000 rupees.

Netherlands

Hacking is defined as intruding on an automated work or part therefore within intention against the law. Intrusion can be considered defeating any security measures, false signals, or false cryptographic keys using stolen usernames and passwords. You can get one-year imprisonment along with a fine of the fourth category.

United States

Any unauthorized use or damage of a protected computer is illegal. A protected computer is a computer that is used by a financial institute or the US government. The computer can also be used in affecting any sort of commerce or commu-nication. The computer does not have to be located in the United States. The maximum imprisonment is one year or a fine that is not more than $5,000.

14 - How to Hack Facebook

Facebook is one of the largest and most popular social networking sites there is. The popularity of Facebook continues to grow, along with gaining new members every day, hackers look closely to Facebook. You will learn and understand the basics of hacking into anyone's Facebook even though you do not possess any real hacking experience.

Before you go getting into someone's Facebook account, you will need to have three fake accounts that your friend is going to add to their account. You will need to ensure that you have access to all of these fake accounts or else your plan is not going to work and you will not get into the Facebook account.

Forgotten password

Open www.facebook.com and hit the "forgot password" option. This will offer you three different options that you can use in order to recover the forgotten password. Choose any one of the options but keep in mind that the first option is going to require that you have the email address to the account. If you choose the second option, you only need to have the username.

The third is the simplest; it requires you to enter your friend's name and your name before selecting search. If you followed the first two steps correctly, then you will see the profile picture for the profile you are trying to gain access to. If this is the correct account, simply click "this is my account." You will be shown the option that you picked to recover the password.

This is where you will tell the interface that you do not have access to the email account. At this point in time, you can create a new email in the form that is provided. You need to make sure that the email you use is not already tied to another Facebook account. You will be prompted to answer their questions that are in place for the account.

If you do not know the answers, then hopefully you can guess right. If you try three times and get it wrong three times, then you are not going to be granted access to the account. If you guessed the answers correctly, then you are going to choose the name of the three friends that are on the profile. These will be the three fake accounts that you created.

After you have done this, you are going to select the continue button. Facebook is going to automatically send a security code to all three accounts. You will need to log into these accounts and get the security code so that you can put it into the form that Facebook provides for the account you are hacking.

You will now be directed to reset the password and give Facebook the new email address that you gave it earlier. After you have reset the password, you now have access to the account.

15 - How to Protect Your Facebook

As noted in the last chapter, getting into someone's Facebook is fairly simple. But, if it is that simple, what happens when someone does it to you? You are going to want to protect your account to ensure that it does not happen to you. And, protecting your account means a lot more than just not giving out your password.

Protecting your account

Make sure that you create a strong password

A strong password will not contain pet names, your name, birthdays, or any other common words that someone can easily guess when attempting to hack your password. The longer your password the harder it is to crack. A password should contain eight or more characters including an upper case, lower case, number, and special character.

Do not use the same password across multiple accounts

This makes it easier for hackers to get into your Facebook and other sites like your email. Using the same password and changing the numbers is not going to give you enough security. A password generator is a good idea if you are having problems thinking of a new password.

Use your Facebook security settings

They can be accessed through your settings under the general tab on your account. After you have gone there, you are going to see a list of settings that you will be allowed to adjust. You can change our password here. You should change your password frequently to protect yourself from being hacked easier.

Use the log in alerts for your account

They are going to let you know when someone who is not authorized has logged into your account. The alerts can be sent to you via mobile or email. Log in approvals are going to be found in your security settings as well. Log in approvals requires a security code when logging in from an unknown browser

Choose trusted contacts

Trust contacts will be given access to helping you get back into your Facebook if you have trouble getting back into it.

Review your apps and browsers

If you see any apps or browsers on your list that you did not give access to your account, you need to delete them so that they do not continue to have access.

Look at what sessions are currently logged on

There is a list that is going to tell you what apps, browsers, and devices are logged into your account and they will tell you the date and location in which it was last used. If something is logged in that should not be, make sure that you end the activity so that you close the session down. To ensure extra security, you can end all sessions that are logged in.

Software and Hardware Keylogger

To protect yourself from others trying to hack into your Facebook from hackers that are using the hardware and software keylogger methods, you need to make sure that you pay close attention to your Facebook because these attacks can often times go unnoticed.

Having a strong password is a must obviously. But a strong

password will not necessarily keep people out of your account. Change your password bi-weekly. Use a password safe. Changing your password is going to render any other password that they have useless since it will no longer work. An example password is: H3rH!ghness

The longer and more complex your password is, the harder it will be for a hacker to guess it. Do not use easy to guess dictionary words.

Keep your firewall on

A hacker that uses keylogging is going to send information through your internet browser to try and gain access to it. Having a firewall in place, it will monitor any activity that is done online and help protect against suspicious activity that may be occurring on your computer.

Keep your firewall up to date. A firewall is meant to keep the viruses and hackers out of your computer, but it is not one hundred percent preventative. Take other precautions so that you keep your computer protected.

Keep your software up to date

If a company finds out that there is a weakness in their software, they work diligently to update it so that there are no longer any bugs and it can push out any suspicious activity The software is updated to keep the user and equipment safe. Be sure to keep everything on your computer up to date or else you are leaving your computer open to an attack.

Install a password manager

Changing your password often can lead to forgetting your password. A password manager will keep your password so that all your information stays safe. The password will automatically be filled into any forms that require it so that you required to type it in.

This helps people who use the keylogging method from finding out the password since you are not constantly typing it in. Web browsers usually offer a password manager

Stealing cookies

Cookies are a used by many websites. Even so, you are going to be able to protect yourself from the people that use them in order to gain access to your accounts.

Make sure that you use a VPN (Virtual Private Network)

VPN will protect you from side jacking (a malicious attack that a hacker uses to hijack a web session using a remote service.) Side jacking can occur when you are on the same wireless network.

No matter what website you are on, your browsing will be safeguarded by a VPN. When using Facebook, your account settings can be accessed by clicking on the security tab.

You are going to be able to make sure that your browsing is secured from there. Firesheep will then be enabled to sniff out any cookies through encrypted links such as HTTPS. Stay away from any site that just contains HTTP in the address.

Stay on Wi-Fi networks that you trust

A hacker could be sitting right next to you and be going through your files and even your email on your computer without you realizing it. If you use a public connection, ensure that your firewall and antiviruses are up to date.

Also, make sure that you do not put your sensitive information out there where hackers can get ahold of it. Use a full-time SSL (Secure Sockets Layer. Browsers like FireFox have add-ons such as HTTPS-Everywhere or even Force-TLS

Be sure to log off any website once you are done using it

If you are logged off, then Firesheep is not going to have access to your account because you are not logged into it.

Phishing

Phishing is mean to make you believe that you are actually on the site even if you are not. You need to be careful about the things that you receive in your email and while visiting websites. Make sure that you are using an anti-virus program as well as a web security programs that will help to protect you against phishing scams.

Norton and McAfee are just a few of the anti-virus programs that you can install and use. Go to Google and search for free anti-virus software. Keep in mind that free versions are not going to allow you to enjoy the full protection benefits that you would if you buy a subscription for the program.

Do not click on any link that is sent to you through email

If the email that you received is telling you that you need to log into your Facebook through a link, then you do not need to click on it without first checking to make sure that the URL is correct. If you are still wary of the URL, then go to the website and log into it the way that you always do.

Hackers are able to make duplicate websites that look exactly like the website that you are always used to logging into. They do this because they know that a website such as Facebook has sent them an email, they assume that it is legitimate and just click on the link and sign in.

Hackers are able to get into your social media accounts and a variety of other accounts because you are not paying attention to what you are clicking on. Pay attention and do not make it easier for hackers to get to your personal information.

Remember that phishing is not done just by email

It can be done through a text message or even in a chat room. When an ad pops up, you need to be cautious because there could be malicious content attached to it. For the ads that pop up, you need to make sure that your ad pop up is turned on in order to try and prevent this from happening. Do not click on anything that looks sketchy and makes you question if it is real or not.

If it begins to ask for personal information, then it defiantly is not something that you need to be putting information into.

16 - Protecting Your Website

The biggest thing that you can do to make sure that your site is protected is to make sure that it is not open to vulnerabilities and that everything is on the most recent version.

Keeping your site up to date

Have a strong password

Make sure that your password is not tied to any other account. Look at the applications that you use on your site, are they absolutely necessary? If you no longer use them, get rid of them. The applications that you do use make sure that you maintain them and keep them updated.

Applications open up a spot that you can be attacked from. The less that you have to keep closed and protected, the lower of a risk you are going to have of being attacked. Keep your browser and any programs like Adobe or Flash updated. The most common attack you are opening yourself up to is phishing attacks that will compromise your workstation.

Once compromised, your usernames and passwords will be compromised as well. Delete data that you do not need. Get rid of backup files that you do not need. Delete log files that are not needed. This will help your site run better and faster. It also leaves fewer access points for a hacker to compromise.

If your site has been compromised

Unpublish your site

Take your site offline so that it cannot be easily accessed by the hacker. The chances are that they already got the information that they wanted.

Go through and make sure that you bring everything up to date

Remove anything that you do not absolutely need on your site. Change your password. Remember that there are multiple ways to get into a website. But there is no way to actually know how they got in.

Contact your website support team for any additional help. If you do not feel comfortable reopening your website. Copy all the information and create a new website. Make sure that you learn from your mistakes.

Cleaning up your website

There are services that you can pay for that will help clean up your site if it gets hacked so that you can restore it to its original working order.

The cleaning process

A forensic team is going to investigate how the hackers were able to get in and compromise your site. They will clean up any infection that they find on your site. You will be provided with an in-depth report on the removal process of any infections that they were able to find when they did their search.

The removal of malware links or malicious code that could be hiding in things like pages and comments. A detailed checklist of how to protect yourself from further attacks. The option of purchasing and installing the program to give you a one-year license and site clearing to help keep you protected from another attack in the future.

17 - Conclusion

Thank you again for downloading this book! I hope this book was able to help you to learn the basics of hacking so that you can apply it to your own life. The next step is to determine if you want to advance your skills to the next level. If you do, then you are going to be able to look for other books on Amazon as well as do your own Google searches that are going to allow you to go to the next level of hacking.

Please remember that hacking is highly illegal and is not encouraged in any way in this book.

Book 1 - Blockchain

A Beginner's Guide To Understanding And Mastering Of Blockchain (FinTech, Bitcoin, Cryptocurrencies, Future Of Money, Data)

1 - Introduction

This book contains explanations on how to understand and master the Blockchain.

This book also explains what Bitcoin is and what it represents as a monetary system and how it is related to the Blockchain.

This book discusses the original Bitcoin Protocol Paper or "whitepaper" written by Satoshi Nakamoto. The original Bitcoin Protocol Paper or simply, the Bitcoin Paper discusses Bitcoin as a peer-to-peer electronic cash system. This is a full breakdown of the Bitcoin protocol, which is intended for those who are interested but still are confused about cryptocurrencies, especially Bitcoin.

You won't be required to know anything about programming, cryptography, or networking. You'll learn everything you need to learn about the Blockchain and the Bitcoin protocol in a nice easy-to-understand explanation.

By the end of this book, you'll understand the brilliance of the Bitcoin Blockchain, the Bitcoin Paper, and the protocol.

Thanks again for purchasing this book, I hope you enjoy it!

2 - Understanding the Blockchain

What is a Blockchain?

You may have heard of the term Blockchain--Blockchain and cryptocurrency. But what on earth is a Blockchain and what does it have to do with Bitcoin?

Bitcoin is the foundation of the Blockchain technology. It is the technology that started it all. Bitcoin is the parent that has spawned children because it is successful. And as a successful technology, it has created a number of other opportunities in FinTech or financial technology.

When people use the term Blockchain they are actually referring to one technology that is part of Bitcoin. It is perhaps the most visible technology that stores transactions, the public ledger, and the list of all transaction that has happened. Also, it is a decentralized replicated database. That is what the Blockchain is.

But most people don't use the term Blockchain to mean Bitcoin. These people use the term Blockchain to mean things that are similar to Bitcoin. Some people use the term Blockchain to mean the things what Bitcoin does and all of the other applications that have nothing to do with money. And as a result, no one really knows what Blockchain really means.

Blockchain is an industry. However, Blockchain, in itself, is meaningless. Blockchain is the term we use to say, "The technology behind Bitcoin," which is a bit like saying, "Network is the technology behind the Internet."

And of course, if you're one of the industries that is being massively disrupted by the Internet, maybe you want to say, "Hey, we can do Network too!"

"We don't want to do the public, messy, open, not-very profitable freedom-bringing Internet, but we can do Network all day. As long as it's private-controlled and profit-making-- we can do Network too."

And if you think that's fiction, that's exactly what happened on the Internet in the 90s. That's what the phone companies tried to do. Phone companies tried to create a "private" internet. It was the Internet without any of the interesting things. It was the Internet where you needed a license, a registration, and an account. And now, a lot of companies are trying to do the same thing with the Bitcoin technology.

So, Blockchain is about things that are interesting, but it is also about things that are not interesting. Not surprisingly, it also means that these are just attempts by consultants to confuse the people so much in order to make more money on the side. But in this book, we're going to focus on the interesting things about the Blockchain.

So how do you tell what a Blockchain is and what it isn't? What are the things that are interesting about Bitcoin? What are the things that are interesting about the Internet? Is the Internet interesting because it offers you Network? Is Bitcoin interesting because it does online payments?

And so, what actually is Bitcoin?

3 - What is Bitcoin?

Well, Bitcoin is a system of payments that is "open." What does "open" mean in terms of cryptocurrency?

It means anyone can access it, anyone can participate on it, anyone can innovate on this system without asking for permission.

It is borderless

There are no borders. Just like there are no borders on the Internet, there are also no borders in Bitcoin. The Bitcoin protocol simply does not see distinctions between countries. The distinction between countries is meaningless in the Bitcoin space.

It is neutral

The Bitcoin doesn't care if the participant is male or female, Christian or Muslim, old or young, rich or poor, brown, black, white or whatever. The protocol doesn't care because it's neutral, it validates transactions whatsoever.

It's a decentralized system

There is no central point of control in the Bitcoin Blockchain.

It is censorship-resistant

You cannot, censor, freeze, or cancel transactions. Those are the things that make Bitcoin interesting. Likewise, those are the things that make the Internet interesting. This is why both the Internet and Bitcoin are so powerful.

Bitcoin alternatives

There are other Blockchains that also share those characteristics of Bitcoin. In fact, people have taken the basic recipe of Bitcoin and in the first year, they have created alternative coins, which are called Altcoins. Since then, more and more Altcoins were created.

Today, there are more than 15,000 Blockchain-based systems that use the basic recipe of Bitcoin. There are variations of that design principle to create systems of currency, systems of trade, platforms, and various other things. These are all Blockchains. Most of them share the interesting characteristics of Bitcoin. They are open, borderless, neutral, and censorship-resistant.

But some of these systems do not have the good characteristics of Bitcoin. Out of the 1,500 Altcoins--90% are worthless. Even worse, more than 90% of those Altcoins are probably scams. Their primary purpose is to enrich the people who created them.

The problem with some people is if they see something successful, they try to create their own.

In fact, we have seen the emergence of a very large number of scams like Ponzi schemes, multi-layered marketing systems, and pyramid schemes.

Bitcoin and cryptocurrency experts would tell you not to try selling Bitcoin to someone. According to these experts, those who don't understand how Bitcoin works should not try to invest on it. This is because the Bitcoin technology is still in its experimental stage.

As an individual, you should devote your time to learning how Bitcoin works. You should focus on the acquiring the technical skills that allow you to turn it into a startup business, a career, or an industry that is innovative.

Avoid turning it into an investment

Stay away from people who want to convince you that the Bitcoin cryptocurrency system is an investment, that it's a sure, safe, and a risk-free investment, or even worse, it is a system that is guaranteed to make you rich overnight. These are the characteristics of all the investment scams that have victimized millions of people around the world.

Remember that nothing in life is easy, risk-free, and will make you rich overnight. Scam coins, Ponzi schemes, and multi-level marketing schemes are very popular in countries, like South East Asia. Those who are entering the investment market for the first time, especially the countries in this region, should avoid these get-rich-quick schemes.

It will not make you rich

In fact, it can make you lose all your savings in an instant. As a system in the experimental stage, it is volatile, and there are risks involved. Bitcoin experts are only recommending that you should completely understand this technology before doing anything else.

This enormously powerful technology should not be used as an investment, especially the kind of investment that involves a higher risk of losing all your wealth.

4 - Bitcoin and other cryptocurrencies

Now, let's talk about the other systems that are out there. There are probably about a dozen other cryptocurrencies. Cryptocurrency is another term we use for these other open Blockchains, these public systems of ledger that can be used to build systems of trust.

Some examples of these cryptocurrencies are Dash, Monero, Ethereum, Zcash, and Litecoin. All of these are cryptocurrencies that are based on open public ledgers. They represent interesting technologies that are developing alongside Bitcoins. There are many other cryptocurrencies that are also growing in popularity today.

Bitcoin experts do not recommend you use those as a speculative investment either. The best thing to do is to understand what they do and how they're different from each other so that you can get a better picture of this industry as it emerges.

Ethereum

Ethereum was based on a paper published in 2013 by then

19-year-old, Vitalik Buterin. The idea behind Ethereum is if we can have this public ledger that allows us to trust and do computation at scale. And instead of using it for money, we use can use it to run computer programs.

These computer programs run everywhere, and their results are recorded in a way that is immutable, persistent, and trustworthy. These computer programs are run by all of the participants. It is a global, secure, decentralized form of cryptocurrency. It has a system of money called ether.

Interestingly, what Ethereum really allows you to do is run smart contracts. The idea here is taking contractual arrangements; the kinds of things we would do in commercial contract law or transactional law as it's known. It also involves encoding relationships and contractual obligations in software programs.

Running a smart contract is the same as the way you would do contract in human spoken language but instead encoding it in software, and then having that program of law execute on the global platform.

Ethereum is not money, but it is a part of this system of

trust that is based on the same global Blockchain phenomenon.

The Blockchain isn't just money

People have suggested using Blockchain for nonfinancial applications, mostly applications that are related to trust. One very common application is the registration of assets or ownership of tangible and intangible things.

For example, and this a problem in developing nations and an area where Blockchain can have a very large impact, is the registration of title over land and the ownership of assets like houses.

The advantage of using a Blockchain is if you record something on the Blockchain, it cannot be modified--it is immutable. Once recorded on the Blockchain, the system of trust prevents anyone from reversing it, from overwriting it, or from changing the past records. And as a result, it creates a permanent, immutable record of transaction history.

In a real estate transaction, this concept is just as important. It allows you to pass off a piece of land from person to person independently, while no one being able to falsify that record or steal your land through paper.

One of the common thefts of land is the falsification of paper. You don't have to go into someone's land with guns and take it from them if you can go to the local land registry office, bribe someone to change it into your name, and send the police into their lands to take it from them on your behalf. That kind of scenario can really be affected by a Blockchain.

The other situations where the Blockchain can be applied for non-financial applications are the registration and access to assets. You can, for example, have the title of a car, a boat, an aircraft, registered on the Blockchain. A Blockchain allows you to record the fact that a transaction has happened and that record cannot be modified or falsified.

So these are elements where the same mechanism that's used to create trust for money and transactions can be used to record the truth, in a permanent, immutable record.

That's the good side of the story...now, let's talk about the bad and the ugly.

That same term, Blockchain, is used to mention a lot of

things that do not have any basis. What has become a trend lately is this idea that you can do Blockchain without Bitcoin. Many people do not want a piece of Bitcoin because they have seen it is a bad form of cryptocurrency. Bitcoin is used by criminals, gamblers, and it degenerates.

One of the fundamental mechanisms behind the Blockchain is its security. Bitcoin allows you to have a system that is decentralized. Without the central point of control, a competition is created in which those who provide security are rewarded in Bitcoin, the currency.

So the currency in Bitcoin is not just the vehicle in doing value transactions, it is the basis of the mechanism of security. And that mechanism of security allows you to have a Blockchain that is operated and secured by anonymous participants whose only claim to provide security, is that they submit as a promise for their security.

These people risk their energy, but they may gain something and as a return, they are given a reward in Bitcoin, the currency.

That competition, that game is the basis of Bitcoin security but what that system of security allows you to do is have the system managed by everyone, so no one is in-charge.

Here's the problem, if you take the system of reward, then there is no mechanism for punishment. If you take away the punishment for cheating, there is no security.

Blockchains use a currency because they use a system of security that is based on market forces on game theory. To use a Blockchain without a currency, you have to find another way of doing security.

If you use a Blockchain in that kind of way, as a private, closed system where trust is assigned to institutions; if those institutions are compromised or their keys are stolen or hacked because you've concentrated all of that power in just a few participants, that system is no longer secure.

These are the same companies that got hacked every time we read on the news. We're supposed to trust the companies to run these Blockchains.

The whole point of Bitcoin's open, public Blockchain is the true system of currency. Bitcoin's Blockchain creates security that does not depend on any individual or institution. If you take the currency away, the security model disappears too, and your back to a ledger that is controlled by a single entity or a few entities.

We actually have a name for that--it's called a database.

So how can you tell the difference between real and not real? How can you tell which cryptocurrency is efficient?

Well, you can ask the following questions as guidelines in distinguishing the most efficient currency.

- Is it open?

- Is it public?

- Is it borderless?

- Is it censorship-resistant?

- Is it neutral?

- Can anyone access it without permission?

- Can anyone use it without permission?

- Can anyone innovate on it without permission?

Is the answer to all those questions is Yes? Then it's giving you the values that we all find interesting in Bitcoin's Block-chain. And you can say that to a number of other cryptocur-rencies and Blockchains as well.

5 - The difference between Bitcoin and the Blockchain

What is Bitcoin and what is the Blockchain? What do these things have at the very core that gives them the characteristics they have? How do you tell them apart? What are the differences between the systems? And what applications do they have?

You should not focus too much on the Blockchain because you could miss the whole point of this technology. In relation to Bitcoin, Blockchain is just one of the several components of this leading cryptocurrency.

This is the crucial issue. Where is the value of Bitcoin derived from? Yes, it is a Blockchain. But it is a very special Blockchain.

Bitcoin is fundamentally open, borderless, transnational, censorship-resistant, etc. Ironically, they are also the things that most critics of Bitcoin point to as its greatest weaknesses.

Bitcoin cannot be allowed to exist if it's borderless and open to access if it has no ability to be controlled. It cannot be allowed to exist. And yet, it exists.

So out of this experiment, this experiment that has lasted 7 years, we now have this really disruptive force that is forcing us to re-imagine what it means to do a payments network. And out of that, we come up with the most brilliant marketing campaign in the history of disruptive technologies.

Imagine if you've invented the new disruptive technology. And you managed within 4 or 5 years to completely distract the incumbent by persuading them to follow in your footsteps and to adopt the central premise of your technology in order to disrupt their own business from the inside out.

But the truth is that the financial services sector, especially the world's major banks took hold on the Blockchain. Why? Because they are looking at the possibility that Bitcoin and some of its elements cannot be disrupted when they are used.

But Blockchain is not the only thing that makes Bitcoin tick. And so, in this effort, we see similarities in the early internet. In the early days, when companies saw the internet, and they saw that it had no editorial control, no centralized security mechanism, no barriers to access.

This represented a terrifying departure from the model of IT. And so as a result, most companies resisted, they built intranets using TCP/IP, and they put heavy firewalls all around to separate those intranets, keep them controlled, give them editorial access and control, and tame the system. They ended up with these islands of stagnant innovation that gradually became less and less secure.

And then we have the second wave of the Internet where many of the most effective disruptive companies in the space took their internal IT infrastructure, turned it inside-out, faced the world, put everything on the Internet, and fully harnessed the collaborative potential of keeping an openly accessible system.

We no longer live in a world of Oracle and IBM. We no longer live in a world of dominance through enterprise computing and enterprise software.

Collaboration is the name of the game. The most robust and secure systems are the ones that are on the internet, subject to attack every single day subject to competitive disruption every single day and through that process they've become robust.

Ironic that 15, 20 years later, we're repeating this conversation with the Blockchain. So, the question is, if TCP/IP isn't the magic sauce, but the really interesting thing is the open-access collaborative global network, does that mean that intranets are useless?

Does that mean that TCP/IP on your land or your data center has no value? The answer is of course not. These are still very powerful technologies. These are still very useful models for adopting?

However, the best thing you can do with an intranet is to interconnect it to other intranets, and for that, you need the internet.

We now realize it had fundamental problems in scaling, in addressing, in routing technology and many other things. And yet, TCP/IP was good enough, at scale with network effect, so fast that it became that it became irreplaceable. In fact, it has become, un-upgradeable. TCP/IP is so embedded into global networking that it resists its upgrades to ipv6, and has resisted to its own upgrades for almost 20 years.

The Internet can't possibly scale beyond Usenet, email, attachments, to voice, to video, to Oculus VR, 3d, 4K, capabilities. It doesn't for a while until it does. And then we shift the goal of what scaling means. And Bitcoin can't scale to Visa until it does. It can't scale to a global transactional network until it does.

But what really Bitcoin can scale to. It can scale to a 7 to 10 billion dollar secure transnational network that remains up and running 24 hours a day, 365 days, for 7 years. It can run without a single successful attack against the core protocol.

Not because there had been no attempts, but because it had been under attack from Day 1, 24 hours a day by some of the most sophisticated adversaries the world has ever seen. Why do hackers attack Bitcoin? It is because Bitcoin has a 7 billion dollar security bounty.

Bitcoin's Blockchain is a system that's on the Internet and lives right there, in the dirt, in the war zone of Internet security and it survived. And as it survives, it gets stronger every day.

So now, if that's what Bitcoin is, maybe it will be the one that becomes the internet of money.

Without any uncertainty, the world of finance will forever be dominated within less than 2 decades by open, global, transnational, censorship-resistant, largely anonymous, and fully encrypted and privacy protected payments network based on the exact model of Bitcoin or Bitcoin with optimizations.

And maybe that thing will be Bitcoin with optimizations. Maybe it will be something unrecognizable that we still call it Bitcoin because we know that branding works. Or maybe we'll call it something else.

The Proof of work algorithm is decentralized with anonymous participants. That is Bitcoin, you cannot change that. Everything else is up for negotiation.

And so now the question becomes, "What are we going to do with Blockchain?" And what's going to happen to the banks? Well, some of the banks will adapt. And Blockchain will have very interesting applications.

Blockchain has certain useful characteristics. As a technology, Blockchain, in general, is not an answer.

Maybe that's what we're talking about. But when you're talking about that what are the limitations of that technology. What does it do and what does it not do? Just because it is Blockchain, it will do everything that you think it will do.

So let's examine some of the nuances. The first is immutability. One of the things that people suggest that Blockchains have as an inherent characteristic is immutability. You can record something on that ledger, and once you record it on that ledger, it cannot be changed.

So how does Blockchain's immutability work? Let's say you want to recreate your version of the transaction history. You will need to present a valid proof-of-work if you want to rewrite the Blockchain. That proof-of-work needs to be properly computed.

Also, you've got to wait for everybody else to stop doing what they're doing while you recalculate the past because they continue moving into the future, creating along their Blockchain while you're wasting your resources rewriting transaction history.

Censorship resistance and Coercion resistance are a representative fact of the anonymity of mining, the decentralized nature of Bitcoin mining.

So the problem is that you can actually coerce the participants in the system to rewrite the financial history of transactions that represent moral hazards of extreme proportions.

The next question is, why would you use such a thing for a settlement system?

SWIFT or the Society for Worldwide Interbank Financial Telecommunication is expensive, it's slow, and it's mired in Geopolitical control. Those equity clearing systems are not as bad but they're still expensive and slow, and certainly, you're directing a lot of profit. Why not just re-implement a banking consortium that does settlement internally?

5 - THE DIFFERENCE BETWEEN BITCOIN AND THE BLOCKCHAIN

One of the things about having a centralized clearinghouse, apart from the fact that they have maximum transactional efficiency, is that they can operate at billions of transactions per second. And the Blockchain can't replicate that level of efficiency, there's no way you can do it. Physically, it is impossible. But let's say you get around that.

So until now, at least, the brokerage game is gained. Front-running, algorithmic trading, dark pools, the futures game is rigged. The foreign exchange game is rigged as well. But at least the settlement game isn't.

Are you going to give that to a consortium of banks to do without any oversight? And you're going to do this with a Blockchain that has what, full encryption? Complete anonymity? Well, that's a double-edged sword.

But if you make it fully transparent then the first time a hacktivist group Anonymous gets into that market and leaks that Blockchain. Every transaction ever made will be exposed. When that Blockchain leaks, the black budgets of some governments will be exposed to a million people.

And how do you protect the keys that are used to sign this

consensus algorithm?

You're creating an enormous concentration of risk there from a security perspective because if those keys are stolen, even just as a denial of service attack, they will lead to disastrous consequences. There is no system in the world that we can design that can keep secret information secret forever.

Bitcoins answer, is to decentralize the power so massively, or as much as possible, that there is no place to press the button, to pull the lever, to exert control, to force the system.

The whole point here is decentralization.

Now, Blockchains can effectively decentralize big parts of the financial system. They will absolutely generate cost savings for banks. They will affect the margins, they will increase efficiency. Like intranets, they will be very useful tools.

6 - Mastering the Blockchain

Bitcoin Paper Broken Down Step-by-step: The Abstract Section Explained

If you spent so much time looking into Bitcoin you probably find yourself being directed to the Bitcoin Protocol Paper or simply, the Bitcoin Paper, which was written by Satoshi Nakamoto. But then you're finding yourself skipping over bits of information and then probably soon giving up completely on understanding it.

This chapter aims to explain each paragraph of each section in the Bitcoin Paper in such a way that it is much easier for beginners to understand Bitcoin, the Protocol, and the whole system.

There are political and philosophical ideas that back up Bitcoin and why you ought to use it. But there are also scientific reasons that prove Bitcoin is the best cryptocurrency today.

Bitcoin's invention, the actual solution or problems that Bitcoin has solved is an incredible feat that many can't still believe it. No other cryptocurrency has done it before. It actually has solved multiple highly complex problems all at once.

But the problem with the Bitcoin Paper is that it is extremely challenging to a typical person or even someone who knows about programming, networking, and cryptography.

First off, the Bitcoin Paper is highly condensed. The full paper describing the protocol is 8 pages long. The 9th page is a reference. This task of writing the Bitcoin protocol down in 8 pages alone is quite impressive. But it proves very challenging to consume for many people.

The goal here is to literally explain everything that someone might not know such as Hash, proof-of-work, and best effort systems.

Here, the problem that we're trying to overcome is explained as well the very brief introductory solution.

If you don't have the paper, you can get it by going to Bitcoin.org/bitcoin.PDF. However, you don't necessarily need the paper to follow along because this book will literally be covering every single topic.

Let's begin by reviewing the first paragraph in the Abstract section from the Bitcoin Paper.

"A pure peer-to-peer version of electronic cash would allow online payments to be sent directly from one party to another without going to a financial institution. Digital signatures provide part of the solution, but the main benefits are lost if a trusted third-party is still required to prevent double spending."

-Bitcoin Paper

Here, we've got the problem and it's discussed. Peer-to-peer electronic cash is obviously the major goal and it would be great if we achieve this. And the reason why is if we could remove the middle man entirely, and doing this creates extreme efficiency in every transaction.

This problem with the middleman, or at least, the necessity for a middleman, is known in Computer Science or mostly in computer networking as Byzantine Generals' Problem. The issue is how 2 or more remote entities can send messages between each other while also know that those messages are authentic and not manipulated in some way.

So in the sense of a large network, how do we know that everyone in that network is working towards the right goal?

Broken down entirely, the problem supposes that, the reason why it's called Byzantine Generals' Problem is that this general or generals are trying to coordinate an attack or retreat on a city. And they're trying to do this with their lieutenants. But the problems is, obviously, this is a co-ordinated attack, you got to be spread apart around the city and you want to get it in on all of the best positions.

The problem is how do we send messages to all of the other groups/armies if we want to attack at a certain time? One problem here is that the messenger himself could be a bad person. Another problem is that there might be conspirators who are planning to turn on the general and misreport the attack or retreat commands.

So how can we ensure that the messages that are being sent between the generals are legit and they haven't been manipulated along the way?

So only until recently, there were just proposed beginnings to the solution and then comes along Satoshi Nakamoto to write an 8-page Bitcoin Paper and blast all these problems away.

Let's review the second paragraph from the Abstract.

"We propose a solution to the double spending problem using a peer-to-peer network. The network timestamps transactions by hashing them into an ongoing chain of hash-based proof-of-work forming a record that cannot be changed without redoing that proof-of-work."

-Bitcoin paper

So now we're going to discuss how the Byzantine Generals' Problem applies to Bitcoin as a peer-to-peer electronic cash system. The main threat to a system like this is the fact that people will lie and people will double spend transactions. These are the traitorous people in the Byzantine Generals' Problem. This can and will cause the network to become corrupt in an instant and make the system worthless.

It is proposed that the network timestamps and logs transactions by hashing them into an ongoing ledger. This ledger is a hash-based proof-of-work ledger which can't be changed without redoing that proof-of-work.

Well, that's a pretty big mouthful and so this is one of the lines that people gloss over. So the first part where people might trip up here is hashing.

7 - Hash Functions

Hash functions are used to generate fixed-length bits of data. It's like a shorthand note that corresponds to the original input. This can be used as a way to store and retrieve data associatively. But in our case, we're more interested in its cryptographic benefits. In cryptography, hashing is used to validate the integrity of data.

With hashing, the identical input will always produce an identical hash. A slightly different input will give a drastically different output. And even if you have the same singular input it's still a vastly different output hash.

Now, let's go on and discuss this notion of hashed-based proof-of-work system. Remember that we are combining the idea of a hash and proof-of-work.

Proof of work

A proof-of-work system is a way to deter threats such as DDos attacks or even spam. But it can also be used for network protection for very similar reasons why it works with DDos and spam, brute-forcing or trying over and over again to break something. With the proof-of-work system, doing these attacks becomes extremely costly.

If you don't know what a DDoS attack is, it stands for Distributed Denial of Service. These attacks are carried out by overloading a network with simultaneous requests. A request, for example, is when you request something from the web server when you want to visit a certain web page.

The idea behind the proof-of-work system is that the actual computational work is required to make a request on the network.

For example, let's assume that the request that we're talking about is indeed visiting a web page in your browser. Since in this case, you request data from the web server, that data is sent to through your browser and then displayed for you.

So if this web page uses a proof-of-work system to deter, let's say, DDos attacks, then each time you visit this website your computer is going to solve a calculation in order to validate its request. So before the web server actually serves some data, it's going to request that you do something for it first to just kind of legitimize yourself.

The idea here is to make the cost of the brute force, DDoS attack, or spam quite high in terms of CPU power, since both brute force and DDoS attacks are usually in like a thousand of requests per minute, per second, or even more.

Without proof-of-work, then it's relatively cheap, initially, to perform a DDoS attack. You can actually do DDoS attack with your own computer and at least send a few thousand requests a second. Most average computers can do this type of attack with no problem at all.

So if you begin to require proof-of-work per request, the legitimate user will likely notice no performance difference. Other people wouldn't even know that you have the proof-of-work system on your computer. On the other hand, the attacker will incur an extremely higher cost and will soon realize that spam, brute force, DDoS and all these threats have become economically less feasible.

The challenge here, however, is making this proof-of-work system asymmetrical. Where it's arbitrary and very simple for the main server and the website to confirm that you got the correct much simpler than it is for you to actually solve it.

8 - Bitcoin Paper

Let's head on to the next paragraph in the Abstract.

"We propose a solution to the double spending problem using a peer-to-peer network. The network timestamps transactions by hashing them into an ongoing chain of hash-based proof-of-work forming a record that cannot be changed without redoing that proof-of-work.

The longest chain not only serves as proof of the sequence of events witnessed but proof that it came from the largest pool of CPU power."

-Bitcoin Paper

When you add hashing and proof-of-work, you have a hash-based proof-of-work. Even further yet, in a very crude way, if you will witness a live hashing or demo on the computer through the Python programming language, you'll see that as the chain gets longer, it gets harder and harder to replicate.

And even identical bits of information in different successions or if you're missing a succession, are completely different.

Over time, the network only gets stronger and stronger. Even though it already started off very strong, as time goes on, it's only getting harder and harder to fake transactions.

In order to fake or change a current block, one would first need to compute every single previous block and redo all of the work contained.

Here is the next paragraph.

"As long as the majority of CPU power is controlled by nodes that are not cooperating to attack the network, they'll generate the longest chain and outpace the attackers."

-Bitcoin Paper

It takes CPU power to generate these hashes. So it's just mathematical certainty that whoever has the most CPU power will have the quickest generation of these hashes.

You could have multiple adversaries trying to attack the network. But as long as they are on their own and not co-operating together, or becoming the majority of the CPU power, they will fail.

So as long as a number of people that are attacking the network are not cooperating together, then the good people would generate the longest chain.

The 51% Attack threat

This basically means that as long as there are legit people or as long as there are more legit people than illegitimate people, then the legitimate people will always outpace the illegitimate people because they are working together.

However, in this case, it is measured in CPU power. And this is why someone, controlling 51% of the computing power of the network can be problematic because they can figuratively run away from the legit people with it.

However, even if someone does reach this 51% of the computing power, he still doesn't have that so many options. This is because the reward for attacking the network is going to be less and very messy than the reward for actually working with the network. So if the motive is financial, then the attack is economically not feasible, it won't make much sense.

Let's say some billionaire wants to attack the network because he thinks he will become a trillionaire if he succeeds, but unfortunately, he can't do it either. It doesn't make fiscal sense. Even if you have that computational power, it just doesn't make that fiscal sense to attack the network, it makes more sense if you work for the network--you'd make more money that way.

If the motive is malicious towards the network itself, let's say that the government wants to take it out. They could stop the network from working, basically. They could use their power to carry on their motive, but executing it is extremely costly. Moreover, it would be impossible to maintain an attack on the network over an extended period of time.

This is what, based on those 51% attacks, makes the Bitcoin protocol incredible. Also, it is because the attack itself can't last, it doesn't make sense if the motive is financial, and it doesn't make sense if the motive is to destroy the Bitcoin network.

Best effort system

The last paragraph of the Abstract reads:

"The network itself requires minimal structure. Messages are broadcast on a best-effort basis, and nodes can leave and rejoin the network at will, accepting the longest proof-of-work chain as proof of what happened while they were gone."

-Bitcoin Paper

A good example of "best effort" in play is with your internet service provider. So, your plan, typically, is your best-effort plan. This means if you have a 50 megabytes per-second-plan, you would ideally get the 50 megabytes per second that you pay for. However, there's no guarantee that you get exactly 50 megabytes per second.

In networking, a best effort system means that there's an attempt to deliver everything but there's no attempt to retry and there's no guarantee.

Another comparison here that's often made in real world terms is the Postal Service's Parcel Post. A sender can send some mail but there's no guarantee that it's going to arrive. And if it doesn't arrive there's no attempt to retry by the system. Nor does the sender know, through the Postal Services System, that the mail has arrived.

Obviously now, you can get things such as delivery confirmation, tracking, etc. But just the most basic Parcel Post from the Post Office is a pretty good representation of what best-effort is.

Bitcoin Paper Broken Down Step-by-step: Introduction section explained

The "Abstract section explained" is extremely important because it's a good overview of what Bitcoin actually is. That section covers the basics of what Bitcoin solves and why it works.

In comparison, this section is the Introduction of Bitcoin, which is really a breeze compared to the things covered in the abstract.

Let's review the first paragraph of the introduction section.

"Commerce on the internet has come to rely almost exclusively on financial institutions serving as trusted third-parties to process electronic payments. While the system works well enough for most transactions, it still suffers from the inherent weaknesses of the trust-based model."

-Bitcoin Paper

Here, it is further explained why there even is a problem in the first place and why it needs to be fixed. More of this issue will be discussed later.

All internet financial transactions are requiring a third-party to mediate every single transaction. This is both in disputes and the actual mediation of the processing of these transactions, which is actually cumbersome to validate on both ends.

While the system does work and people accept it, it's actually flawed in many ways.

Let's continue with the second paragraph.

"With the possibility for reversal, the need for trust spreads. Merchants must be wary of their customers, hassling them for more information than they would otherwise need.

A certain percentage of fraud is accepted as unavoidable. These costs and payment uncertainties can be avoided in person by using physical currency, but no mechanism exists to make payments over a communications channel without a trusted party."

-Bitcoin Paper

This original Bitcoin Paper does not actually attack any entities, currencies, central banks, etc. The paper takes no stance at all. It's merely a scientific proposition for efficient transactions. But part of the efficiency, safety and all that is in the fact that merchants do not need to get all these personal information on people.

However, with regulation, that's exactly what will end up occurring because people are afraid that criminals are going to use it to launder money or continue to do their illicit activities with Bitcoin.

With the reversibility, the right of the US dollar, for example, the need for an entity that can be trusted becomes greater. The need for someone to actually act as a middleman in various transactions becomes greater. Anyone selling goods has to vet their customers.

This is incredibly apparent, for example, if you actually try to buy Bitcoin, you usually have to wait 3 to 5 days by a bank transfer, and most places won't even take PayPal. The ones that do come into play in the next sentence, which says, "A certain percentage of fraud is accepted as unavoidable."

You can actually buy with PayPal on websites like LocalBitcoins. However, you have to pay a massive increase over market, which is usually as much as 50%. So that gauges vaguely for you.

How much fraud and risk is there if people are given the opportunity to reverse their payment for a non-reversible anonymous asset? Doesn't that make you feel warm and fuzzy inside?

If you have dealt with PayPal disputes, you may already know the drill. You get a chargeback, you got screwed, and that's it. Very rarely are you able to win a chargeback dispute with PayPal unless you have a lot of information about the transaction with you.

All of the information collection is unnecessary if you use cryptocurrencies like Bitcoin. Also, if you consider websites like LocalBitcoin, where PayPal is accepted, it is unnecessary that people pay a 50% markup in order to fund the scoundrels that pilfer from the system.

On the other hand, we have seen what happens when there is no trusted third party to mediate--hell breaks loose. People scam their hearts out; the markup, information, costs, and everything goes up.

But that's the idea of the Bitcoin network; we can do transactions without any trusted third party involved. There is no need to regulate the Bitcoin because it is self-regulating.

Let's move on to the next paragraph.

"What is needed is an electronic payment system based on cryptographic proof instead of trust, allowing two willing parties to transact directly with each other without the need for a trusted third party. Transactions that are computationally impractical to reverse would protect sellers from fraud and routine escrow mechanisms could easily be implemented to protect buyers.

In this paper, we propose a solution to the double-spending problem using a peer-to-peer distributed timestamp server to generate the computational proof of the chronological order of the transactions. The system is secure as long as honest nodes collectively control more CPU power than any cooperating group of attacker nodes."

-Bitcoin Paper

So that wraps up the introduction paragraph of the Bitcoin protocol. There is nothing new here 'though the actual problem of why the current system is so greatly inefficient is covered and clearly explained here than in the Abstract section.

In conclusion, in the Abstract, the introduction, and in the entire paper, Satoshi Nakamoto (the person or the group), never actually assumed any sort of political positioning. The purpose and goal for Bitcoin was just for efficient transaction--it's just doing things the right way.

Bitcoin Paper Broken Down Step-by-step: Transactions Section Explained

Here's the first paragraph about Transactions from the Bitcoin Paper.

"We define an electronic coin as a chain of digital signatures. Each owner transfers the coin to the next by digitally signing a hash of the previous of the previous transaction and the public key of the next owner and adding these to the end of the coin. A payee can verify the signatures to verify the chain of ownership."

-Bitcoin Paper

Now, keep in mind that this is just verifying the chain of ownership.

So here, we have our first definition of a coin. A transfer of a coin is done by a digital signature in the form of a hash. And so, this is a chain of these digital signatures.

The only part people tripping up on is this notion of a public key. So, what is a public key?

Now, whenever you hear public key, that means the person, at least in the sense of encryption, is referring to an asymmetrical encryption system. In an asymmetrical encryption, you have 2 separate keys where you've got a private key and a public key. These keys are different from one another but they are linked mathematically.

The public key is used to encrypt data, and on the other hand, the private key is used to decrypt any data or to create a digital signature.

So at the end to of all of this, as someone being paid in Bitcoin, you can verify that the person who is paying you in Bitcoin has actually acquired that Bitcoin and they did (or do) own it.

You can verify this by searching for their public key signature at the end of that coin's digital signatures list. These coins have their list of digital signatures.

Now comes the kicker. Let's proceed to the next paragraph.

"The problem of course is the payee can't verify that one of the owners did not double-spend the coin. A common solution is to introduce a trusted central authority, or mint, that checks every transaction for double-spending.

After each transaction, the coin must be returned to the mint to issue a new coin, and only coins issued directly from the mint are trusted not to be double-spent. The problem with this solution is that the fate of the entire money system depends on the company running the mint, with every transaction having to go through them, just like a bank."

-Bitcoin Paper

The problem is, not only is the most recent "owner" able to double-spend that coin at multiple entities at this point. They might pay you in this coin, you examine it and it looks okay, so you believe that this person owns this coin.

But what's to stop them from going to 5 other people and being like, "Hey! I want to pay you with this coin?"

So at this point, you're still being able to show them that you own that coin. If this process was allowed to continue and multiple people along the way could have double-spent that coin, this would obviously be multiplying the monetary supply.

Generally, the answer is to introduce a third party here. The task of this third party is to confirm that each transaction is legitimate and not a form of a double expenditure. And when the confirmation is done, they will then issue a "new" coin.

The only trusted version of money is the one that came from

the central authority. But of course, as discussed in the Abstract and the Introduction, the problem here, inherently, is that a central authority is required to do this where every transaction must go through them.

Let's move on to the next paragraph.

"We need a way that the payee to know that the previous owners did not sign any earlier transactions. For our purposes, the earliest transaction is the one that counts, so we don't care about later attempts to double-spend."

-Bitcoin Paper

The idea here is that the first expenditure is the only one that needs to be tracked as all the other ones are fraudulent. But of course, how do we know which one comes first? But mostly, we just need to understand that the idea of the system is that the first one is the real one.

The next paragraph goes,

"The only way to confirm the absence of a transaction is to be aware of all transactions. In the mint-based model, the mint was aware of all transactions and decided which arrived first.

To accomplish this without a trusted party, transactions must be publicly announced, and we need a system for participants to agree on a single history of the order in which they were received. The payee needs proof that at the time of each transaction, the majority of nodes agreed that it was the first received."

-Bitcoin Paper

Here, we first want to confirm the absence of a transaction. So we want to know there's no previous version of this transaction that's already been done. In the case of the central authority, they usually have a massive ledger, 'though this is not a public ledger.

So to make it work with this system, we would need all transactions to be broadcast publicly and then we actually need another system where the participants of this network agree on a single history of the order in which transactions were done.

The payee needs proof at the time of the transaction. The majority of the nodes in the network agree that this is indeed the first transaction of its kind.

So the way that the payee that can prove this is when everyone shares this massive ledger, the person can ask the network which is the first one. So now, in the form of how will we actually do transactions, we have an answer.

But sadly, this answer needs more work because we do need a way to verify that the transaction has not been done already. So for this, we have a proposal for this time server. A time server is the hash-based time server that was discussed in the Abstract section.

Bitcoin Paper Broken Down Step-by-step: Timestamp Server/ Global Ledger Explained

The problem with transactions is we have a way to do them but we have no way as of yet to confirm that the transaction itself was not double-spent, nor the previous transactions in this chain of transactions.

We can confirm that the person owns, or at least, owned a Bitcoin. But we have no idea if they went to multiple parties and spent that coin multiple times.

So here's the beginning of that solution, and that is a Timestamp Server.

So let's go ahead and hit this short paragraph.

"The solution we propose begins with the Timestamp Server. A Timestamp Server works by taking a hash of a block of items to be timestamped and widely publishing the hash, such as in a newspaper or in a Usenet post.

The timestamp proves that the data must have existed at the time, obviously, in order to get into the hash. Each timestamp includes the previous timestamp in its hash, forming a chain, with each additional timestamp reinforcing the ones before it."

-Bitcoin Paper

The idea here is we can timestamp transactions each time we do it, or doing transactions right. And basically, it's going to enforce the previous stamps. It's like, more agreement on the previous stamps.

So if you think about like any transfer you've done in Bitcoin, you've probably seen that it takes something like three confirmations to be validated. So this means that your transfer has been agreed on. Another block is made, and then another block is made, and so on, depending on how many confirmations are required.

And by this point, you solidify your transaction in the Bitcoin Blockchain and it's also widely agreed upon.

The problem is, however, what if someone decides to take the chain, and just edit the chain quickly and pass it along. Then what happens?

So, sadly as we've resolved one problem, we've presented ourselves with another. Luckily, there's a solution and you probably already know that solution if you paid attention or have read the Abstract section.

Bitcoin Paper Broken Down Step-by-step: Proof of Work Explained

The problem we had so far is we have a way to identify the current and previous owners of a coin but we have now way of knowing whether or not they have double-spent that coin. The solution to this is to have just this massive timestamp server/ ledger that literally logs everything.

And then everyone is made aware of this through broadcasting it to each other and the longest version of this is the accepted one, as it is, you know, the longest one is the newest and also will be the one that supported by the most CPU power/ nodes in the network.

So, with the solution, how do we stop people from actually just editing that log and then passing it along.

This is where Proof-of-Work comes in.

Now let's go ahead and begin with the first paragraph.

"To implement a distributed timestamp server on peer-to-peer basis, we will need to use a proof-of-work system similar to Adam Back's Hashcash rather than newspaper or Usenet post.

The proof-of-work involves scanning for a value that when hashed such as with SHA-256, the hash begins with a number of zero (0) bits. The average work required is exponential in the number of zero (0) bits required and can be verified by executing a single hash."

-Bitcoin Paper

So let's discuss what Hashcash is because it is almost identical to what Bitcoin uses. Hashcash is the solution to the problem most typically of either eMail Spam or Distributed Denial of Service (DDoS) attacks. It is basically the solution to a problem of the attack against a system by making a lot of requests being sent by the attacker.

The name's intention, Hashcash, is to literally convey the idea that it uses hashing to introduce a sort of "charge" for something. So the issue is that, with spam filters, generally spam filters catch non-spam emails in their nets and the result of legitimate emails. In a sense, this is similar to seeing an unavoidable amount of fraud as just being part of the system.

What Hashcash does is introduce a CPU or a processing cost to engage something. Again, this was mostly used in email or in DDoS attacks. For example, when an email is sent, it must first solve a problem, which costs a bit of CPU. For the typical user, the difference is absolutely tiny and they probably don't notice that it is being done.

But to a spammer, the difference is massively compounded, since the spammer might be able to natively send, let's say, 10,000 emails a minute.

Now, with Hashcash, this becomes near impossible without extremely using a high-powered CPU. By that same token, while the puzzle is challenging and at the same time quite costly to the computer that's being asked to solve the puzzle, the puzzle needs to also be very quick to verify using the server.

Generally, Hashcash uses SHA-1, where Bitcoin uses SHA-256. The only reason for this is because SHA-2 wasn't out yet when the time Hashcash was developed.

Bitcoin's proof-of-work system also needs to allow for more fine-tuned version of hash difficulty because Bitcoin actually modifies it slightly.

The way Hashcash works is basically looking for a number of accesses and as you increase the access it goes on multiples of itself. So each time you make it a little more difficult, you can't, you literally have to double the difficulty.

With Bitcoin difficulties, there's a built-in functionality that gauges how quickly new blocks are being developed. And it will automatically make them more difficult to develop if too many are being made too quickly. And so this is how Bitcoin's coin count is easily projected over time and Bitcoin, as a system manages its own inflation.

And this is also why so many people call Bitcoin deflationary since its popularity is not identical to its supply. So no matter how many miners come into play, the supply will stay the same. Bitcoin's popularity and the miners have increased dramatically while the supply is structured. So, mining popularity goes up, challenge rises, and price rises because it's costing people more money to mine Bitcoin.

Let's go back to how Hashcash works.

You have a sever which presents a "challenge" to the requesting computer. The requesting computer is then tasked with taking that challenge and using it. Let's say, as a starting point, and adding characters to the end or appending them to the end of the challenge string.

For example, if the challenge string is "abq 38t". The requesting is then tasked with adding just random text such as numbers and letters to the end of this so for example, "abq 38tyui". Then the requesting computer generates a hash of this. Remember that Hashcash uses SHA-1 while Bitcoin uses SHA-256. So with Bitcoin, a SHA-256 hash is generated with this random bit of text.

Next, to solve this challenge, the generated hash, with Hashcash, needs to start with X (unknown) number of zeros (0). Basically, it's just a matter of chance, which increases in difficulty as the required number of zeros (0) increases.

So the best way to solve this challenge is, literally, to do what's called "brute force". Here, letters and numbers are just randomly added to the end of the string, hashed, and then checked to see if they have the required amount of zeros. If not, they repeat the process and they do it over and over until finally that they've achieved the required amount.

So with Hashcash, it's the number of zeros. For example, going from 5 zeros to 6 zeros results in "double the work." The same thing if you go from 3 to 4, that's also "double the work."

Now, with Bitcoin, it is required that there's a bit more

granularity in the ability to change. And so the difference with Bitcoin is that the Bitcoin protocol uses what are called fractional bits. For example, if you require 4 hex zeros (0), that would be 16 bits because each hex digit is 4 bits.

Aside from fractional bits, the Bitcoin protocol also does what's called the double SHA-256. So what it does is take a SHA-256 hash of a SHA-256 hash of whatever there is to hash.

Now, the concept is really the same. And why it works is totally the same. But with fractional bits, you're basically looking for 5 zeros (0) at the beginning, now you're looking for a hash that's valued at less than one-half to the power of how many zeros (0) you're looking for.

For example, if you're looking for 5 (0) zeros, in Bitcoin, you're looking for a hash value at less than one-half to the power of 5.

In the end, it's really just a very slight variant to Hashcash. Therefore, the idea of Hashcash, or any proof-of-work, is to require a lot of CPU work to find an answer to something that takes a tiny fraction of that same power to verify that it's correct.

Let's continue with the paragraph.

"For our timestamp network, we implement the proof-of-work by incrementing a nonce in the block until a value is found that gives the block's hash the required zero bits.

Once the CPU effort has been expended to make it satisfy the proof-of-work, the block cannot be changed without redoing the work. As later blocks are chained after it, the work to change the block would include redoing all the blocks after it."

-Bitcoin Paper

So, what is a nonce? In general, a nonce is a word that is only used once. In cryptography, a nonce is there to protect against "replay attacks". Replay attacks are where an attacker will re-transmit good data with bad data.

What a nonce is just kind of arbitrary or it's random, and it's appended to the end of whatever you intended to hash. If somebody tries to reuse that same nonce, it's going to result in failure because each nonce must be unique.

This means that each time that you attempt something, you've used that nonce--it's done. So if you supply with the Bitcoin network, basically, it's asking you for an answer plus the nonce that equals what you're looking for.

Therefore, the nonce is there to make sure that every time someone wants to redo or fake that block, he would have to redo that work. And then, any block after it, he would also have to completely redo that work. This is because they wouldn't be able to use the same answer in the same nonce because the same nonce will be rejected.

The only way to fake blocks that have already been gone through would be to redo all of the CPU work. This is why, as the chain grows, it solidifies the previous transactions. And also, this is why 3 confirmations on the network are thought to be absurd and that's fine.

If you did the math, it would literally cost billions of dollars in computer equipment and about 10 million dollars per minute just to fake the network.

So let's continue with the next paragraph.

"The proof-of-work also solves the problem of determining

representation in majority decision making. If the majority were based on one-IP-address-one-vote, it could be subverted by anyone able to allocate many IPs. Proof-of-work is essentially one-CPU-one-vote. The majority decision is represented by the longest chain, which has the greatest proof-of-work effort invested in it.

If a majority of CPU power is controlled by honest nodes, the honest chain will grow the fastest and outpace any competing chains. To modify a past block, an attacker would have to redo the proof-of-work of the block and all blocks after it and then catch up with and surpass the work of the honest nodes.

We will show later that the probability of a slower attacker catching up diminishes exponentially as subsequent blocks are added. To compensate for increasing hardware speed and varying interest in running nodes over time, the proof-of-work difficulty is determined by a moving average targeting an average number of blocks per hour. If they're generated too fast, the difficulty increases."

-Bitcoin Paper

Now, here, the most important point of this last paragraph is basically the last 2 sentences where Bitcoin inflation controls are described. Here, many people accused Bitcoin as highly deflationary and that it is a bad form of currency.

Well, Satoshi Nakamoto, the creator or Bitcoin, set into place rules that Bitcoin would not go into any form of hyper-inflation. Even if Bitcoin became extremely popular, very fast or even in the case of computer hardware, becoming much more advanced than anybody could ever predict.

Although people can predict how fast the average computer might be in 10 years, still, it's not that easy to do. So, instead, it's not how much power is required, it's built in how many blocks can be achieved per X amount of time.

So, if suddenly, the number of Bitcoin miners wants to double, or triple that actual output of Bitcoin, in the block's mind, would stay exactly the same. This is because the difficulty of Bitcoin mining would increase to match this.

So what ends up happening in Bitcoin, as the Bitcoin difficulty goes up, CPU cost goes up, and electric costs and all that. So, either price will go up to match it, if demand is there. Or miners won't be able to continue and they would drop out. And as they drop out, the difficulty will fall. This lowers the cost and justifies the mining.

This basically ensures that people will always be there not only to mine and be incentivized to mine but also incentivized to be highly efficient and competitive.

In all of parts or sections in the Bitcoin Paper, this is what astonishes Bitcoin experts the most. Because even if a bunch of people started mining Bitcoin, the supply wouldn't come too much too fast and just crush Bitcoin prices. So despite its volatility, it's actually not that risky as compared to other things to maybe some other things that you might be able to invest in.

Bitcoin Paper Broken Down Step-by-step: The Network Section Explained

This section is an explanation of the Bitcoin Network setup. Despite the scary and ominous-sounding name, this is actually a piece of cake compared to the Proof of Work section.

Let's review the Bitcoin Paper's step-by-step guide to run the Bitcoin network,

"The steps to run the network are as follows:

1. New transactions are broadcast to all nodes.

2. Each node collects new transactions into a block.

3. Each node works on finding a difficult proof-of-work for its block.

4. When a node finds a proof-of-work, it broadcasts the block to all nodes.

5. Nodes accept the block only if all transactions in it are valid and not already spent.

6. Nodes express their acceptance of the block by working on creating the next block in the chain, using the hash of the accepted block as the previous hash."

-Bitcoin Paper

So, in Step 1, the paper says that every transaction that's done is broadcast, which again, is on a best effort basis.

Step 2, each node collects new transactions into a block. Obviously, we're logging all the transactions that have occurred in the newest block.

Step 3, while doing step number 2, each node is working and finding that proof-of-work for that block.

Step 4, when the node finds the proof-of-work successfully, it's going to broadcast the block to all the nodes. This is more like one big announcement. And again, this announcement is on a best effort basis.

Step 5, nodes will accept that new block but only if all the transactions within it are valid and not pre-spent transactions.

Step 6, acceptance of a block is expressed by these nodes when the nodes begin working on a new block. And basically, they show their acceptance of exactly what block they accept because they are including the hash of that previous block in the new block.

As explained in the Timestamp Server section, the timestamps are hashed and each new block contains the previous block's hashed timestamp, which includes every other previous block's timestamp.

If you hashed the same input in the same order, you would end up with the same exact hash. So you still only have that 1 hash, but in theory, it contains every other hash within it, which is based on that order of input.

Let's continue with the next paragraph,

"Nodes always consider the longest chain to be the correct one and will keep working on extending it. If two nodes broadcast different versions of the next block simultaneously, some nodes may receive one or the other first.

In that case, they work on the first one they received, but save the other branch in case it becomes longer. The tie will be broken when the next proof-of-work is found and one branch becomes longer; the nodes that were working on the other branch will then switch to the longer one."

-Bitcoin Paper

This is another example why the "best effort" is the chosen system. As a rule, nodes choose to accept the longest chain because this is the chain that clearly is the most supported by the most CPU power in the network, since, to be the longest it has to have the most "CPU votes", so to speak.

In the case of 2 nodes broadcasting at a new block at the exact same time, some nodes will get one version, other nodes will get another, and they will both work on achieving the next block.

Now, whoever reaches the next block first would be the victor, and the nodes working on the other one would simply shift over because, again, at the broadcasting of a new block, the nodes will realize that they are working on a shorter, invalid chain and they would just jump over to the new one.

Let's proceed with the last paragraph,

"New transaction broadcasts do not necessarily need to reach all nodes. As long as they reach many nodes, they will get into a block before long. Block broadcasts are also tolerant of dropped messages. If a node does not receive a block, it will request it when it receives the next block and realizes it missed one."

-Bitcoin Paper

Again, the best effort system is further utilized here. This also builds on the previous paragraph where, simultaneously, 2 blocks for broadcast and the winner is the one where the proof-of-work is solved first.

So if a block is missed, or if somehow did not get that message, the nodes are going to keep working on the previous block and once another block is received, that node that is behind will realize that it's working on the wrong chain and will automatically try to catch up.

So why is the best effort system used here?

Again, if you skipped the Abstract section, best-effort means there's an attempt to do something, but if that something doesn't occur either it's done wrong or whatever, there's no re-attempt, there's not error reporting and any of that and everything just keeps trucking along.

So the main benefit to a best-effort system is a lot like the main benefit to the Bitcoin network itself. Moreover, it's a lot like a type of "machine learning" called an "artificial neural network". This kind of a network contains a principle known as "graceful degradation". The attempt of this network is to mimic the human brain.

For example, you have a task and you give the artificial neural network a picture of a couch. Now, some of the nodes in the network might call a futon, a few other nodes might call it a bed, and many going to call it a chair. There's a possibility that many of the nodes are corrupt.

But, hopefully, the majority of the nodes will say that it is a couch. And if the artificial neural network is working correctly, the couch will obviously have the most votes. So this is why "graceful degradation" is useful and why neural networks within this logic of parallel programs are really helpful.

On the other hand, when you normally have what's called linear programming, which is literally a step-by-step process on a single line. The problem here is if any of the steps along the way gets messed up, everything automatically fails. With linear programming, you either succeed or you fail.

Fortunately, with "graceful degradation", networking, and parallel programming, the task given will be completed successfully. Even if it's a multiple tasks and happening at the same time or multiple calculations, and some nodes can be wrong, some will fail, but as long as the majority is correct-- you'll find yourself having success with completing the task.

A good analogy here is between a rope and a chain. So in a chain, if one of the links is broken, the whole chain is rendered useless. But, with the best-effort system, neural networks, or parallel programming, you've got something more like a rope where some individual fibers might break and yet the rope itself is still in one piece, it still is successful.

Now, in Bitcoin, with voting, processing, and working on new blocks--it's all parallel programming on a best-effort basis. So even when some nodes either get corrupt, mistakenly or purposely send and get the wrong data--it won't matter. The Bitcoin network itself is based on "graceful degradation", it will still be going to operate correctly and securely.

Bitcoin Paper Broken Down Step-by-step: Incentive Section Explained

So what is the incentive to support and work with the network? As well as what's the incentive, for example, if you have a lot of computing power to overpower the network. And, what's the incentive of either working with the network or overpowering the network?

So, let's go ahead and start reviewing the first paragraph of the Incentive section from the Bitcoin Paper.

"By convention, the first transaction in a block is a special transaction that starts a new coin owned by the creator of the block. This adds an incentive for nodes to support the network and provides a way to initially distribute coins into circulation since there is no central authority to issue them.

The steady addition of a constant of amount of new coins is analogous to gold miners expending resources to add gold to circulation. In our case, it is CPU time and electricity that is expended."

- Bitcoin Paper

Here, initially, it's explained that the incentive to be a part of the network is to acquire coins as a reward. And, this is also the chosen method of coin distribution in the network. In addition, this is compared to people who are using resources to mine, let's say, gold. The main cost here is obviously the CPU, time, and electricity.

So then, the question here is, "What happens in the year 2140?"

In 2140, all of the coins will be mined for Bitcoin. And so no coins will be awarded at this point for supporting the network.

But what if we don't even reach 2140 before a number of miners in the network slows down?

Let's continue with the next paragraph.

"The incentive can also be funded with transaction fees. If the output value of a transaction is less than its input value, the difference is a transaction fee that is added to the incentive value of the block containing the transaction. Once a predetermined number of coins have entered circulation, the incentive can transition entirely to transaction fees and be completely inflation free."

-Bitcoin Paper

So the idea here is to eventually move to a peer transactional cost system. Despite the standing which is a lot like the current system we're in, where we've got 2 people that want to transfer money, and we've got a middleman that we've got to pay--this is not quite the same, this is still very much like peer-to-peer and the transactional cost would be a flat fee.

First of all, your money is not going to filter through a third party, so to speak, it is still into a going peer-to-peer basis. However, you'll still need that middleman to be some sort of a notary confirming that a real transaction has taken place and that there are 2 real people involved.

Moreover, the transactional cost would most likely be a flat fee rather than percentage-based. With Bitcoin, we're talking probably 1 to 3 dollars to make a transfer.

Right now, competition for mining all and this is extremely high for people to acquire coins. But when coins are no longer being distributed or if they begin to lose value, the actual hash difficulty will drop. So, whether or not 500,000 miners or just 50,000 miners, you're going to notice relatively similar results when it comes to transactions speed and all of that.

The only threat here is that if the number of miners was to actually drop, someone could easily come in and execute a 51% attack. At which point, the question is, would it still not be worth attacking the network?

Before we answer that question, let's look at the last paragraph first.

"The incentive may help encourage nodes to stay honest. If a greedy attacker is able to assemble more CPU power than all the honest nodes, he would have to choose between using it to defraud people by stealing back his payments or using it to generate new coins.

He ought to find it more profitable to play by the rules, such rules that favor him with more new coins than everyone else combined, than to undermine the system and the validity of his own wealth."

-Bitcoin Paper

So here's why the 51% attack doesn't really make that much sense, even if someone had the resources. There's more incentive to actually work with the network. If the incentive is just plain malicious such as to kill the network or something, this would prove to be a costly endeavor. So, neither of those options is a good one.

Now, this is where the question is asked whether the Bitcoin network will still be as secure as it is today by the year 2140.

And by secure as in relative to the day's mining power. Most Bitcoin experts agree that there is less certainty about security as mining will be more about transaction fees rather than actually acquiring coins.

The takeaway here is, at least right now, there is a large incentive to mine Bitcoin. As we already know that the difficulty of mining is systematic and it changes based on a number of miners who are mining at the moment.

So it will always be the case, at least in the year 2140, that it's going to be more fiscal sense to mine Bitcoin for the network than to attack the network.

Bitcoin Paper Broken Down Step-by-Step: Reclaiming Disk Space Explained

This section is actually basic but the diagram and the vocabulary might be daunting to people who are unfamiliar with Bitcoin and cryptocurrency. The goal of this book, especially this section, is to simplify this section as much as possible.

The main idea here is compression. So how can we have all these transactions occurring, requiring everyone to be aware of the full Blockchain history and transaction history, and yet also keep this digestible and usable?

So with that in mind, let's go ahead and review the first paragraph.

"Once the latest transaction in a coin is buried under enough blocks, the spent transactions before it can be discarded to save disk space. To facilitate this without breaking the block's hash, transactions are hashed in a Merkle Tree, with only the root included in the block's hash. Old blocks can then be compacted by stubbing off branches of the tree. The interior hashes do not need to be stored."

"A block header without transactions would about 80 bytes. If we suppose blocks are generated every 10 minutes. So 80 bytes x 6 x 24 x x 365 equals 4.2 megabytes a year. With computer systems selling with 2 gigabytes of ram as of 2008, and Moore's law predicting current growth of 1.2 gigabytes per year storage should not be a problem even if the blocks headers must be kept in memory."

-Bitcoin Paper

As you already know we are able to verify blocks because if you keep hashing input, the order of the input is exact and so the same input will yield the same output. We can use this concept not only for security but also for condensing things. Using the Merkle trees, we can remove the unwanted parts of all the last transactions.

Bitcoin Paper Broken Down Step-by-Step: Simplified Payment Verification Explained

Let's go ahead with the first paragraph of the section.

"It is possible to verify payments without running a full network node. A user only needs to keep a copy of the block headers of the longest proof-of-work chain, which he can get by querying network nodes until he's convinced he has the longest chain, and obtain the Merkle branch linking the transaction to the block it's timestamped in.

He can't check the transaction for himself, but by linking it to a place in the chain, he can see that a network node has accepted it, and blocks added after it further confirms the network has accepted it."

-Bitcoin Paper

Here, if you're being paid in Bitcoin you would need to wait for node confirmation, which is what you typically see in transfers where you 're waiting for X confirmations, and new blocks after, which also further solidifies the transfer in the agreement. Typically you're waiting for 3 confirmations or something like that.

Let's continue with the last paragraph.

"As such, the verification is reliable as long as honest nodes control the network, but is more vulnerable if the network is overpowered by an attacker. While network nodes can verify transactions for themselves, the simplified method can be fooled by an attacker's fabricated transactions for as long as the attacker can continue to overpower the network.

One strategy to protect against this would be to accept alerts from network nodes when they detect an invalid block, prompting the user's software to download the full block and alerted transactions to confirm the inconsistency. Businesses that receive frequent payments will probably still want to run their own nodes for more independent security and quicker verification."

-Bitcoin Paper

Now again, this is where the 51% attack comes into play. If the majority of the CPU power is conspiring to lie, then the network is obviously no longer secure. If a 51% attack was used, then this simple method would be easily fooled and one would want to instead have the full Blockchain.

The way someone could be tipped off here is if there is, let's say, some agreement among the nodes and it's a notification or alert that could be thrown out. And you could then download the full chain yourself and see what the inconsistency is and all that. Or you could just wait until there's no more alert or notification.

There are definitely a lot of things you can do here. You can have various security measures taken into place to see if there are multiple competing Blockchains. The whole idea here is that the accepted Blockchain is the longest Blockchain.

Bitcoin Paper Broken Down Step-by-Step: Combining and splitting Value Explained

This section of Combining and Splitting Value is mostly just here to clear up what some people might be worried about and one of these is how do we handle varying amounts of Bitcoin that are transacted.

Up to now, it really only been discussed in the idea of like a whole coin each time and obviously we can split up a Bitcoin and trade multiple fractions of a coin at a time. And that's the part that makes Bitcoin so brilliant -- it is very divisible.

Let's start by reviewing the first paragraph of the Combining and Splitting Value section from the Bitcoin Paper.

"Although it would be possible to handle coins individually, it would be unwieldy to make a separate transaction for every cent in a transfer. To allow value to be split and combined, transactions contain multiple inputs and outputs. Normally there will be either a single input from a larger previous transaction or multiple inputs combining smaller amounts, and at most two outputs: one for the payment, and one returning the change, if any, back to the sender. "

-Bitcoin Paper

This section is basically there to just quickly dispel any fears about how the system might be worthless since you wouldn't be able to easily combine or divide a payment. The idea here is you can have multiple inputs for a transaction and you're usually having 2 maximum outputs. The goal here is that everything is cleaned up in a nice fancy way.

So to track a payment, you wouldn't have to figure out where that money fully came from, since you could consider this as an exchange where when you buy 1 whole Bitcoin, you might get a 0.2 from a person, 0.5 from another person, and 0.3 from yet another person, and after that, you might sell only 0.7, and so on.

Naturally, as time went on, let's say you sold 0.7 to a guy who's buying a 1 whole Bitcoin as well, so he gets 0.7 from you, 0.2 from another guy, and 0.1 from another guy.

As you can see, things could get messy in an instant, which is why you might be required to have a full transaction history in order to keep up with what has been going on.

Bitcoin Paper Broken Down Step-by-Step: Privacy Section Explained

Bitcoin and Bitcoin protocol privacy is kind of a hot topic issue because there are also many misconceptions surrounding it.

In some ways, Bitcoin is more anonymous than your typical online money methods. But in another way, it's actually more public. In the end, it really comes down mostly to the user's choice. Users can decide where along the spectrum they wish to be.

Now, the government will tell you that this is a matter of national security and terrorism, and so people can be private about their finances, but in reality, your privacy is your freedom. But remember, criminals also seek privacy just like law-abiding citizens do.

So, how does privacy in Bitcoin work? And is this even an issue?

With that in mind, let's review the first paragraph of the Privacy section of the Bitcoin Paper.

"The traditional banking model achieves a level of privacy by limiting access to information to the parties involved and the trusted third party. The necessity to announce all transactions publicly precludes this method, but privacy can still be maintained by breaking the flow of information in another place: by keeping public keys anonymous.

The public can see that someone is sending an amount to someone else, but without information linking the transaction to anyone. This is similar to the level of information released by stock exchanges, where the time and size of individual trades, the "tape", is made public, but without telling who the parties were."

-Bitcoin Paper

So here, you can see from the typical model that identities are tied to transactions, which go through the trusted third-party and then end up at the counterparty. Unfortunately, the public is, basically, not informed about this at all.

In the Bitcoin protocol network model, identities are the separate part. The transactions basically go through the public in the form of a ledger.

Let's move on to the last paragraph.

"As an additional firewall, a new key pair should be used for each transaction to keep them from being linked to a common owner. Some linking is still unavoidable with multi-input transactions, which necessarily reveal that their inputs were owned by the same owner. The risk is that if the owner of a key is revealed, linking could reveal other transactions that belonged to the same owner. "

-Bitcoin Paper

Now, here's the important part where the user gets the right to choose their anonymity level. In the case of a charity, for example, they would likely, if they were legitimate, opt to use the same public key.

This is, by the way, only for all donations and expenditures. The reason here is for the public to see where the donation money was going. This is an organization that should be very transparent, which is an easy way for people to do.

A corporation has much competition, would probably choose the secret route, or an anonymous route. This means they would change their public key very often so that it would be harder to track where money is being spent.

Now, obviously, they would still be required to report their earnings to the government for taxation purposes and things like that.

Interestingly, this option for anonymity is where the debate is. Businesses and organizations now have a basic way of doing it. People and businesses that have a level of security invested in being private also have also had a basic way of doing so.

Moreover, these options can even be married for a perfect balance that you or your business can choose. You can have your public funds in one location. This is the stuff that you don't really mind if people see. And then you can have some private finances that you don't want you don't want the public to be aware of how much you have or what you spend your money on.

Now, with all of that said, when concerning these matters of national security, terrorism and things like that, tracking Bitcoin is easier than tracking most online payments, and it's definitely much easier than tracking cash payments.

If one tries really hard, he can relatively filter through all the payments and eventually start linking accounts. He can make a "tree", and if he has a few accounts. He can start using the process of elimination and get rid of accounts, and then he can then start finding out who exactly owns what.

True anonymity is difficult to get away with on this public ledger. So far, some of the most anonymous minded people in the Bitcoin space still had failed.

In conclusion, many Bitcoin experts think there's no problem with this added degree of privacy. It is simply just a new model, which is not necessarily more private than the last.

Bitcoin Paper Broken Down Step-by-Step: The Conclusion Section Explained

The Conclusion is the last section of the Bitcoin Protocol Paper.

Here is the paragraph of that section.

"We have proposed a system for electronic transactions without relying on trust. We started with the usual framework of coins made from digital signatures, which provides strong control of ownership, but is incomplete without a way to prevent double-spending.

To solve this, we proposed a peer-to-peer network using proof-of-work to record a public history of transactions that quickly becomes computationally impractical for an attacker to change if honest nodes control a majority of CPU power. The network is robust in its unstructured simplicity. Nodes work all at once with little coordination.

They do not need to be identified, since messages are not routed to any particular place and only need to be delivered on a best effort basis. Nodes can leave and rejoin the network at will, accepting the proof-of-work chain as proof of what happened while they were gone.

They vote with their CPU power, expressing their acceptance of valid blocks by working on extending them and rejecting invalid blocks by refusing to work on them. Any needed rules and incentives can be enforced with this consensus mechanism."

-Bitcoin Paper

Quite possibly the most powerful line is the last line in the paragraph. This really what opens the door to pretty much anything, including Bitcoin's evolution. Likewise, changes to the Bitcoin protocol can be made. The Bitcoin protocol is an open source code, which means anyone can edit that code and pass it along. And as long as the nodes support it, it can be passed along.

Most importantly, the combination of rule changes is what's voted or not. If nodes don't support it, it simply won't pass. Remember, it's one CPU, one vote.

However, this also has some implications because it's not one person, one vote--it is CPU power. Therefore, you could assert that this voting system favors the wealthy who can afford to buy more CPU power.

The wealthy who are indeed supporting the network with their money should get that extra voting power. Nevertheless, there could also be wealthy people who choose not to support the network as much but want to get that voting power.

Bitcoin as money is just the first medium that is exchanged over the Bitcoin protocol. You can actually exchange anything over the Bitcoin protocol such as contracts, money, cars, or businesses. This protocol can be used for any mode of transfer and any forms of voting.

9 - Conclusion

I hope this book was able to help you to fully understand and master the Blockchain.

The next step is to know more about the Bitcoin Blockchain by learning new topics such as Hash Pointers and Data Structures, Digital Signature, Distributed consensus, Bitcoin scripts and their Applications, Bitcoin blocks, P2P Blockchain network, Limitations & improvements, etc. There are also a handful courses on the Blockchain that you can find on the internet.

Book 3 - Big Data

A Beginner's Guide To Using Data Science For Business (Transforming Information, Deep Learning, Boost Profits, Business Intelligence)

1 - Introduction

Filled with current information and practical guidance, this book will show you how to:

- Nurture an information-focused culture, and allow your organization to develop fresh tactical and operational plans based on valuable insights

- Determine what business areas to digitize and how best to use raw data to convert them into information that is valuable for your organization

- Find the best way to analyze the data you have collected using the current and future tools and technologies in Big Data

- Establish the right security and privacy measures to safeguard your organizations from data breach

Big Data is gradually changing our society, especially the business landscape. This book is a practical guide to make sure that you don't only survive, but stay ahead of the game.

2 - A Short History of Big Data

About 90% of all data in recorded human history has been only generated in the last decade. But the need to use and understand data has been around for centuries, even millennia. As a matter of fact, Mesopotamians have been discovered to use early forms of accounting to keep track of their herds and crops.

The use of accounting has gradually improved, and in the 1600's, Great Britain used a far more complex system to record and examine all information about mortality rolls in London. The early statistician John Graunt wanted to understand and build a sophisticated warning system for the Black Death that ravaged Europe.

Graunt recorded the first example of statistical data analysis where he archived his discoveries in his book Natural and Political Observations Made upon the Bills of Mortality. This book offers better understanding on the causes of death during the 1600s. Graunt is regarded nowadays as the father of statistics because of this great work.

During the 1800's, Information Age flourished in Europe and in the Americas. In 1887, modern data was first gathered by Herman Hollerith who invented a computing machine that is capable of interpreting holes punched into the paper cards to organize data for a census.

During the time of US President Franklin Delano Roosevelt, the country pioneered a significant data project to monitor the social security contributions of employees across the US. The US government commissioned IBM to develop a machine for the significant task.

During the World War II, the United Kingdom developed the first data processing machine designed to decipher codes intercepted from the Nazi. The device was called Colossus, which had the capacity to search for patterns in codes at 5000 characters p/s.

It was a breakthrough invention as it significantly reduced the time needed to complete the task -- from weeks, even months, to merely hours and even minutes.

The United States National Security Agency was created in 1952, and after only a decade, it has secured contracts with around 12000 cryptologists. The agency was tasked the monumental undertaking of interpreting information during the Cold War as they began automatically gathering and decoding intelligence reports.

In 1965, the American Government funded the project to create several data centers to archive 172 million sets of fingerprints and 742 million tax returns. The task required data specialists to transfer all files into magnetic computer tape and keep them in one file location.

However, the project was discontinued over privacy protests from the public, but it signified the start of the era of the digital data storage.

Tim Berners Lee, a British computer scientist, invented a network of data sharing system, which was eventually known as the World Wide Web. The system was designed to host share information through the hypertext. This invention paved the way for changing how the world consumes data.

Starting in the 1990's, millions of data was generated at an unprecedented rate as more and more people need to be connected to the web. The first supercomputer was developed in 1995. The computer has the capacity of performing calculations in a second compared to an ordinary calculator used by one person could in 30,000 years.

The Era of Big Data

The term Big Data was coined by Roger Mougalas of O'Reilly Media, which was the company who coined the term Web 2.0. Mougalas used this term to refer to a dataset that can be impossible to organize and process using conventional tools for business intelligence.

At the same time, Google created MapReduce on top of Yahoo's Hadoop, which both aimed to index the whole web. At present, many organizations around the world are using the open-source platform of Hadoop to interpret large data sets.

As more platforms appeared including social networking sites, the rate of data creation increased rapidly. Soon, startups started mining this vast amount of data and governments also started funding data projects. In fact, in 2009, India funded a massive data project to store all fingerprints, pictures, and iris scan of its 1.2 billion citizens. This massive data is stored in the largest biometric database in the globe.

According to a 2-11 report published by McKinsey entitled

Big Data: The Next Frontier for Innovation, Competition, and Productivity, by 2018, the US will need around 200,000 data scientists and about 1.5 million data managers. Hence, the role of Big Data Scientist is regarded as the most in-demand job today.

As a response, more and more Big Data startups appear to help organizations manage and make sense of big data. As businesses are now gradually adopting Big Data, similar to its welcome gesture in 1993 for the Internet, the revolution for Big Data is still ahead of us. Hence, we are expecting to see a lot of changes.

As a matter of fact, the volume of data is growing fast at such unprecedented rate that we just can't use the old decimal point system. Nowadays, US agencies like the FBI and NSA are now using yottabytes, in computing their data volumes.

In the next couple of years, we might start using brontobytes to refer to sensor data. Basically, new terms are being coined to refer to the volume of data that is projected to be generated in the future.

Societies and organizations around the world will be completely changed by Big Data. Data scientists project that the volume of data that is currently available will be doubled every two years.

In the next Chapter, we will take a closer look at what Big Data exactly is and why it is crucial for business organizations.

3 - The Importance of Big Data in Business

Basically, anything that is digital is considered as data. Today, current software and hardware cannot handle the vast volume of various forms of data being generated at such unprecedented pace.

Big Data has become too dynamic and too sophisticated for conventional tools that we have today. It requires complex tools for effective processing, storage, analysis, and management. The volume of data that we are facing is so vast that our software and hardware technologies are lagging behind to keep up.

However, data scientists also developed tools and technologies to make sense of Big Data so they can be used for specific purposes. The insights gained from this information could be used to aid business decisions, enhance efficiency, increase sales, and decrease costs. Big Data has become a significant element in modern business, and it has changed the landscape across industries.

4 - The Seven Vs of Big Data

Experts explain Big Data through the Seven Vs - Volume, Variety, Velocity, Value, Visualization, Variability, and Veracity. We will discuss these elements in detail:

Volume

At the current rate that data is being generated, the volume is expected to double every two years. Around 1.8 zettabytes of data were created in 2011, and according to a study published by the IDC, by 2020, the whole world is projected to create 50x this volume of data.

This rate is staggering, and a major catalyst to this hyper-expansion is the IoT or Internet of Things, which is mainly from sensors installed on different devices that generate data continuously.

For example, modern farms generate and collect high volumes of data from the sensors added to the tractors. Farm equipment such as John Deere is installed with sensors to regulate the expanding fleet of their farming machines, keep track of their machine optimization, and thus helping farmers make informed decisions.

Meanwhile, modern airplanes are now capable of generating about 3 billion terabytes of data every year from the sensors added in the engines. Oil companies are now using sensors to search for more oils in wells, which generate around 10 exabytes of data.

Only decades ago, this massive production of data would result to significant problems in business operations. Today this is not a major concern any more thanks to the cheaper cost for data storage and improved storage technologies.

Variety

In the business setting of the past, data was all structured in form, which could all fit into rows and columns.

Today, around 90% of data is not confined in structures as there are many new formats such as structured (flat files, HTML5, log files), unstructured (Binary Large Objects, content management data, digital assets), complex structured (XML based MISMO, semi-structured (metadata tags, RSS feeds, EDI documents), and many more.

Every form of data requires a different form of evaluation and different form of tools for interpretation. Data from social media such as Tweets or Facebook posts or comments can give you valuable insights on customer perception about your brand.

On the other hand, data from sensors provides valuable information on how a specific type of machine or product could be used and also offers insights on how you can further improve your goods or services.

Later in this book, you will learn the different forms of analyses that you can use according to the different types of data and what tools you can use.

Velocity

Velocity refers to the speed at which data is generated, analyzed, stored, and visualized. During the years when batch processing was still the prevailing norm, it is imperative for the database to be updated every week, or if not every night after regular business hours.

Servers and computers need a significant amount of time to perform data processing and database updating. But today, data can be created near real time, if not real time. With the emergence of devices that can be connected to the Internet, it is possible for the data to be updated the moment they are generated.

The rate at which data is presently generated is really surprising. In only a span of one minute, 200 million emails are sent, 100 hours of videos are uploaded on YouTube, 20 million photos are viewed, 2.5 million search queries are performed on Google, and 300,000 tweets are sent.

The main challenge that business organizations are currently facing is how to adapt with the unprecedented rate of data generation that we have right now, which you can learn in this book.

Value

All available data can be valuable not only to business organizations but also to consumers and communities. Big Data can lead to big business, if the organization knows where to look and what to look for. Based on the study by McKinsey published in 2011 states, the possible yearly consumer surplus could reach around $600 billion in 2020 from using personal location data.

The potential yearly value of Big Data for the healthcare industry is around $300 billion, and it can provide more than €250 billion for the public sector administration in Europe.

Of course, we are not talking about the value of data itself, but how organizations could use data for their advantage. The real value here is the analyses performed on the data and how the data could be transformed into valuable information that the business can use in different forms and purposes.

The real value of Big Data is in how business organizations are using the collected data to build information-centric businesses that rely their decision-making on the insights from expert analyses.

Visualization

Visualization is regarded as the core of Data Science because this refers to making sense of the massive amount of data. By using the right form of visualization, raw data can become valuable data for the organization.

Of course, when we speak of Data Visualization, we are not just merely referring to pie charts or bar graphs. We are talking about sophisticated graphs, which involve numerous data variables with the objective of making the data readable and understandable.

Even though data visualization might not be the most difficult task for a data scientist in terms of technological area, it can be argued as one of the most challenging. It can be difficult to transform raw data into a graph to tell a story. Fortunately, there are startups that have emerged in the recent years to help business organizations to visualize their data.

Variability

Variability is an encompassing element in Big Data. Watson, the supercomputer who won the Jeopardy game, demonstrates great variability, which is difficult because words have various meanings based on the context used. In order to provide the correct answer, Watson should understand and make sense of the context.

Some people refer to variability pretty much the same as variety. This is a misconception. If an ice cream shop sells 10 different flavors of ice cream, that is variety. But if the same flavor of ice cream tastes and feels different everyday, then that is variability.

Therefore, variability is quite significant in running sentiment analyses. The definition may change rapidly because of variability. In similar Facebook posts, a word could have different meanings. In order to run a proper sentiment analysis, the system should run proper algorithms to decode the precise meaning of a word in its context. This feat is extremely difficult even for a super computer.

Veracity

There is no point in collecting and analyzing data if it is not true. Flawed data could result to major problems for business organizations and their consumers. If a business wants to be information-centric, it should make certain that the data and analysis are genuine.

This is most particularly crucial when it comes to automated decision-making where human interference is minimal or even zero. If you want to develop your Big Data strategy, it is important to make sure that the raw data is accurate. You will learn more about this later in this book.

5 - Important Aspects of Big Data for Business

After comprehensively defining the essence and meaning of Big Data, it is now time to understand the most important aspects of it that your business must have a good grasp. In dealing with Big Data, a business should be open for changes. Understanding these realities will help the business to continuously adapt to the ever-changing landscape of the business world.

Big Data Is Not All about the Volume of Data

Although the name suggests massive, Big Data is not always about the volume of data involved. On the other hand, some people also think that a Big Data Strategy is only significant for business organizations who are handling petabytes of data. This is not true.

Big Data is beyond the mere collection of a massive volume of data. It is more about integrating various forms of data sets in various variances at various moments from various sources. Specifically, this is about integrating and analyzing various data sets to provide an organization with insights that are fresh and valuable.

Hence, Big Data can also be beneficial even for small and medium businesses. Even if a business is not dealing with petabytes of data, it can still gain more insights if the data is integrated with, for instance, social data or public datasets.

Moreover, Big Data also refers to the analysis of available real time data and using a certain algorithm to project outcome. Insights received on real-time can be valuable for organizations, as it will get a peek on what its customers may do in the future.

6 - Governments Are Now Into Big Data

Aside from business organizations, governments around the world are also producing more data, mainly because of digitization initiatives. For example, Netherlands aims to become completely digital and ditch all paper correspondences by 2017. Just think about the volume of data that will be generated by 20 million citizens in communicating with the Dutch government.

Meanwhile, the US government also allocated $200 million to fund more research into Big Data and how it could help government agencies make sense of its collected data. In order to manage and store the data that the government collected, the NSA has started building a huge data storage facility in Utah, which has the capacity of storing 12 exabytes of data.

Because of these efforts, public data categories will become more available for business organizations, and this could boost innovation and fresh solutions for global problems. More private initiatives are also being introduced year after year to collect private and public data sets for organizations.

This area requires more progress but it is certain that governments could also take advantage of the opportunities in the field of Big Data.

Privacy Will Become an Issue with Big Data

In the era of Big Data, technologies and tools will have the capacity to monitor everyone, like the popular Big Brother. For example, the PRISM leak released by Edward Snowden in 2013 revealed that individual privacy will be affected by the digital age.

Moreover, when the data is not properly concealed, re-identification will always be there as a risk. Even though it takes a lot of time, computational power, and money to achieve re-identification, it is always possible. Moreover, it is crucial to make certain that the data is attributed to its proper owners. Hence, there is a need to manage data properly.

Gradually, people are becoming more aware of the volume of data that businesses are collecting about them everyday. For example, companies are now storing data for as long as three years, which they can sell anytime they like. Most businesses will always try to maximize Big Data.

Big Data Requires Big Security Measures

Businesses that are collecting huge datasets should add a layer of protection to avoid the information getting into the wrong hands. Many large companies who are dealing with private data such as Evernote and LinkedIn have been hacked by online criminals.

Security breach also threatened Yahoo! and Bitcoin in the past. Hence, it is critical to safeguarding all data that is gathered by a business. There are various methods for data security such as encryption.

If your business is willing to harness the power of Big Data, you must also have a crisis plan on standby if in case your servers got compromised. However, only very few businesses have a solid plan in case of security breach, which can be a disaster for the business and for its customers.

It is even more disastrous that only very few businesses have the technology to detect if their data sets are compromised. Hence, businesses must have a plan to thwart a possible hacking. Ignoring the need to protect your data could spell the end of your business.

Data Professionals Will Be In Demand

Based on a report by McKinsey, there will be a shortage of around 190,000 data engineers in the United States as early as 2018. The report also projects a shortage of 1.5 million data managers who are capable of supervising data engineers and could link the IT aspect of Big Data with the strategy for business. Hence, Big Data professionals will be high in demand in the near future.

However, Big Data engineers and managers are not the only people needed by business organizations. There is also the demand for big data analysts, data architects, and of course the rarest – data scientists.

Specifically, Big Data scientists will be the most difficult to look for, and so, expensive to hire. This is actually regarded as the "sexiest" job today, and at present, only few people can really be certified Big Data scientists.

In order to avoid passing up on the opportunity to secure developments in the future, businesses must begin training their IT department on Big Data technologies, especially, if they like to develop Big Data engineering training to prepare your personnel for the future.

As a matter of fact, many colleges and universities are now offering study programs and specializations on Big Data. There are also online courses offered through Coursera and Udemy to help people around the world study Big Data.

Big Data Can Be Found Everywhere

Remember, everything that is digital is considered as data. Every day, millions of files are being digitized and linked to the World Wide Web. Hence, your business may receive new data from totally new areas.

For example, the Internet of Things or IoT shows that any device or product could be linked to the Internet and hence, generate data. Businesses must use this information and should be open for digitizing products and services.

The IoT is a breakthrough innovation as it can turn anything into data. For example, you can add several sensors to a mug to analyze the when someone drinks coffee, where, how fast, and for how long.

If you gather and properly evaluate the data about how the mug is used, you could convert this information, which can be used to make sense of mug use habits of your consumers. Of course, this is a bit light use of Big Data, but the point is, this is now possible.

However, you must also begin looking on the public data marketplaces that are beginning to appear even in places we usually don't expect. These data marketplaces gather paid and free public and open datasets from around the globe. If your own data is integrated with these new existing datasets, your business will gain access to new information and fresh insights.

People Are the Real Drivers of Big Data

Even though a cultural transformation is crucial to take advantage of all the opportunities of Big Data, the actual development of Big Data strategy is really driven from the people behind your business.

Specifically, executives and managers must understand the essence of Big Data and how it could be used for the business. The business should encourage more people in the organization to be aware of the advantages of Big Data for the business so the strategy will be developed and implemented.

It is important to take note that IT must not be solely assigned for Big Data strategy. Remember, the IT department is merely a tool to attain your Big Data strategy. However, it should not be assigned for strategic planning.

To initiate the development of Big Data effectively, the business should start looking for the right advocates inside the organization, particularly as the cost could be high and the ROI during the early stages are not guaranteed.

The ideal sponsor or advocate is a board member or a senior manager, as these executives have the responsibility and the authority to support the initiative even if the initial phases are may seem not rewarding.

Big Data Calls for a Different Culture

In order to genuinely take advantage of Big Data, your business should become an information-centric organization. This paradigm shift could lead to more data-driven decisions, and can provide your employees the chance to develop new tactical, operational, and strategic plans according to the real data instead of calculated risks.

Big Data culture calls for personnel who are encouraged to gather data at specific touchpoints. They should know how to ask the right questions and answer them with the right type of data. Of course, it is really a challenge to change a company culture, but this book will serve as your guide to help you in building a company that is information-centric.- Current Trends in Data Science

Many various aspects of Big Data could affect your organizational strategy, and how your business must deal with it. Remember, every type of data will affect what type of analysis you need to do and what tools you need to use.

Many of these factors include the technicalities of Big Data, but current trends will also affect your strategy and also affect your business as a whole. Hence, it is crucial to take a closer look at these aspects.

Big Data On-The-Go

We need to look at how the data on the go is changing the landscape. The emerging use of handheld devices is boosting the sales of smart phones and tablets. Based on a report released by Canalys, around 1.5 billion mobile phones sold will be smartphones. Moreover, the rise in tablet sales is becoming massive. Handheld devices require a different strategy in dealing with Big Data.

On-the-go big data could be a breakthrough innovation in many areas such as healthcare. For example, doctors may be more efficient if they can carry their tablets or mobile phones so patient information will be more available at the bedside or at the operating room. The mobile age has come and this will call for a different strategy by businesses.

Basically, on-the-go Big Data refers to the storage and visualization of analyzed Big Data on handheld devices such as smart phones or tablets. Analysis cannot be performed on mobile devices; hence, this trend is all about providing consumers and businesses access for information. This may be presented as an easy task, but this involves numerous challenges.

For example, the current trend of Bring Your Own Device or BYOD can be enticing for employees and business, but it can pose some risk for the IT department. Also, employees are encouraged to bring their own devices to work rather than receiving one from the organization. With this rising trend, businesses will also need to take a closer look on their security measures and productivity guidelines.

However, it can be difficult to project the future of mobile Big data as we are still at the brink of mobile innovation. Some experts suggest that our future will be flooded with more handheld or wearable devices with each type requiring a different approach. Businesses will have to adapt on time to meet the needs for mobile.

7 - Real-Time Big Data

Real-time Big Data offers the most value for organizations. The capacity to make sense of petabytes of data from different sources can be interesting and could offer your organization a lot of insights. However, making sense of petabytes of data when they are produced anywhere in the globe can provide even more insights.

Data that is processed, analyzed, stored and visualized in near real-time or even real-time will enable your business to see what is happening among its products, processes, machines, staff, customers anytime and anywhere. If you can easily respond to a movement in real-time, it will be more likely that the organization can benefit.

With massive volume of data available, it will be beneficial to use this the moment it is produced. Real-time analysis could see a huge increase in the future, as this provides many benefits. The capacity to make sense of the attributes of a visitor to your store may increase your sales.

In the age of fast information, getting access to real-time Big Data could become the difference between your business and your competitors. Hence, more businesses may look to base their decisions on real-time information.

Therefore, the collection of data is one thing, and the capacity to analyze, store, and visualize data is another game field. Real-time information can provide your business the capacity to completely understand what is going on inside and outside your business.

The advantages of harnessing the power of real-time big data include instant detection of errors in the organization, immediate visibility of new strategies from your competitors, significant improvement of your service, immediate detection of fraud, increased revenue, cost savings, improved sales insights, and getting ahead of the customer trends.

Real-time analytics also has its flaws, as there are also challenges that businesses should overcome. For instance, real-time analytics requires customized computer. The basic version of Hadoop, at present, is not yet recommended for real-time analytics. There is a need to develop new tools and technologies to better improve real-time access and visualization of data.

Employing real-time insights need a different approach for

business organizations. If your business usually receives insights once a week or even once a month, which is the norm in most businesses, getting insights every minute or even every second calls for a different strategy and different way of working.

Rather than responding on a weekly basis, an immediate response based on real-time data is now crucial. This will definitely have an effect on the organizational culture. The goal must be to make your business information-focused.

8 - The Internet of Things (IoT)

The Internet of Things (IoT) is possibly the largest trend today in Big Data. In the near future, the number of devices that will be integrated with sensors can increase to over a trillion.

Another significant trend is the emergence of quantified self, which enables the consumers to understand what is going on. Consumers also like to know what they are doing and how they could improve their behavior.

In the near future, we might need to refer to brontobytes of data when we discuss the data coming from sensors. IoT, also known as Machine-to-Machine (M2M) communications will enable billions of devices to be connected with each other, and so produce a massive volume of data.

It is estimated that in 2020, 40% of all data generated in the world will be from IoT. Of course, this data should be processed, analyzed, stored, and visualized before it can make sense for the business.

IoT will also enable refinements in the present business paradigms, and it could also open up completely new business models. IoT is already becoming ubiquitous and there is no way to stop this.

Your business can start small with IoT data, as it could easily expand to significant proportions. Start with a prototype, and build on it gradually. Organizations that are flexible with the scope of the project and expand accordingly have the highest chance to become successful.

But the business should always plan from the start to eventually become strong in supporting massive datasets so the project will emerge successfully.

There are endless possibilities with the emergence of IoT. Our societies could become smarter and smarter every day as ordinary things could be intelligence, interlinked, and accessible online. There is enormous potential and there is vast potential use for this trend.

In order to get ahead of the competition, and to keep your customers well taken care of, consider about what IoT and the gathering of big sensor data could do for your business. Consider the products you have and how you could transform these products into sources of valuable raw data.

9 - The Quantified Self

Even though Big Data is usually referred to as being beneficial for businesses, it will also become valuable to individual customers in their personal data. More and more quantified-self programs and applications will enable customers to store, monitor, visualize, and make sense of their own lives.

Information about sleeping, eating, and physical activities could be available, along with records of your life. This is only a matter of years before there will be applications that will integrate all the data from these separate apps into one Big Data app about how you live your life.

Soon, these apps could mash it up with geolocation information from your handheld devices as well as your activities on social media. There are also apps that allow you to compare your performance with your friends.

These quantified-self applications have the advantage of generating a massive volume of data, which will allow you to track information about the whole population groups. This might raise some issue on privacy, but more and more individuals are happy to learn more about their own lives that they are signing up easily.

The concept of quantified self has been around during the 1970's, but it only took off thanks to IoT and the existence of monitoring devices, which can be connected to handheld devices. These devices carry all types of sensors, which could monitor almost anything.

Most technologies on quantified self are focused on improving health and attitude. Hence, most devices are helping individuals to monitor their sleeping habits, emotions, activities, stress levels, food consumption, caffeine consumption, smoking, and much more.

Hence, the movement is targeted towards people who are completely fine with having their personal information gathered, and made available for public access with a certain degree of anonymity.

Big Social Data

In the last few years, organizations have seen the benefits of harnessing Big Social Data, because of the fact that it contains important information that will enable them to better understand their audience or consumers.

Through sentiment analytics, business organizations could

learn what their customers are thinking of their products, services, advertisements, announcements, promos, and more.

Moreover, all accessible social data could be used to run predictive analytics about what customers may like and when do they like it. According to the feedback customer post on social media, businesses could gather insights that will normally call for expensive conventional research.

Organizations that are using information available on social media channels could start hypertargeting customers. Hence, instead of just targeting possible customers by a specific age, gender, or location, businesses could now focus on customers according to their latent or actual needs. All of this data can be derived from what customers say on social media – the retweet or the like and their context.

For example, Walmart is using the information shared on Facebook and Twitter to send personalized coupons to possible customers. It also keeps track of what their customers are commenting – the moment someone tweets about, let's say flowers and chocolates, Walmart can send a discount coupon for those products at the nearest branch.

Another example of hypertargeting is being practiced by MyBuys that provides multi-channel personalization for on-line stores and consumer brands.

The goal here is to improve engagement, drive conversions, and increase sales through the analysis of the individual behavior of their customers, which is no easy task as they have 200 million customers who have generated 100 terabytes of data and still growing.

10 - Public Big Data

In 2011, the Vice President of the European Commission Neelie Kroes introduced some proposals to legally access the data produced and stored by public institutions in Europe. Kroes believe that getting access to these datasets can double their worth to about 70 Billion Euro because when data is integrated and converted into information, it could provide added value to the economy.

The open data portal highlights transparency, innovation, and open governance. The available data could be reused, integrated, analyzed and visualized for commercial or personal use. This is a significant leap forward as it could create new business opportunities and could drive innovation.

Other governments are also considering similar action. For example, Netherlands has already developed a portal on which open datasets could be funded publicly for anyone's consumption.

Netherlands actively supports local authorities and departments in sharing their datasets on this portal to boost innovation and business opportunities. This is believed to result to a more transparent and more efficient government.

Meanwhile, the United States is also now looking into the opportunities on Big Data. Former President Barack Obama introduced a Big Data project worth $200 million to look into Big Data technologies and opportunities.

The goal is to advance available tools and technologies to effectively process, access, analyze, store, and visualize the massive volume of data generated by the local, state, and federal governments.

Australia also developed their own public strategy on Big Data, with the goal of making information held by regional or national authorities available for the public. Australia developed this strategy to make certain that business organizations and governments can take complete advantage of all Big Data benefits alongside securing privacy of their citizens.

11 - Gamification

Much of the new data will be generated from gamification, which in business is not only an effective tool for marketing campaigns, but can also revolutionize the manner organizations communicate with their audiences. It will also create valuable Big Data that could improve big database of businesses.

Gamification refers to the use of game elements in non-game contexts. This could be used to communicate with customers and enhance marketing efforts that could lead to more revenue.

Gamification is also usually used within the organization to improve employee productivity and crowdsourcing initiatives. Ultimately, gamification could also change the consumer behavior. The quantified-self movement is an ideal example of the integration between Big Data and gamification.

The usual gamification elements that are usually tapped in gamification are challenges, leaderboards, avatars, badges, points, awards, and levels. Furthermore, gamification could also be used to learn something, to achieve something, and also to stimulate personal success.

The objective is to enhance real-life experiences and make people more willing to perform something. However, gamification is not all about gaming, but merely the application of gaming elements in a different context.

Various aspects of gamification offer a lot of data that could be analyzed. The business can easily compare the performance of users and understand why some groups are performing compared to other groups. When customers are logging in through the social graph, a lot of public data could be added to provide context around the data from gamification.

Aside from the various elements that offer directly accessible insights, gamification could also help in understanding consumer behavior and their performance. For instance, how long do various groups take to finish a challenge or how do they use specific services or products. Gamification data could be used to enhance your offerings.

Gamification can also be used to motivate people to act and to encourage them to share the right data for the right context. As a matter of fact, gamification must be considered as a catalyst for sharing. The higher user engagement, the more chance they will share. This could lead to more attention to the company as well as more valuable information.

Using gamification for your big data strategy will largely depend on the speed and quality of the information that is returned to the user. Users will be more involved if the content is also better. Big Data can also be used to personalize content. Buying behavior, the time needed to do specific tasks, and engagement levels could be integrated with public data like posts or tweets as well as user profiles.

This will provide your business with a lot of valuable insights if the data has been stored, analyzed and visualized. But, users are now expecting immediate results and feedback. Hence, real-time data processing is quite crucial.

A few years from now, gamification will become more integrated with how consumers are accessing and consuming data. This will result in more data generation. With Big Data, businesses will also need to learn how why their consumers are behaving in the context of gamification, and so, this will provide more insights on how their consumers are behaving in real-life.

This information is quite valuable for marketing and sales department to reach out to potential consumers using the right message in the right context and with perfect timing.

Business organizations should create the ideal design for gamification strategy to gain the desired insights and results. Based on a report by Gartner, 80% of the gamification solutions may not deliver the intended results because of flaws in the design. Remember as with Big Data, flawed design will only result in flawed data and poor insights.

12 - Big Data Technologies

In order to stay competitive, business organizations should take a closer look on the adoption of Big Data in their strategy. It is also crucial to consider the impact of Big Data on your IT, as it also requires the use of new technologies. These technologies may range from various ways of data storage and processing to the different new forms of analyses that could be performed on data.

The Big Data platform is expanding so fast that it can be a challenge to fully make sense of the market and to identify which players could solve certain problems. Because of the potential benefits of Big Data, many Big Data solution providers are now offering possible solutions to those problems.

Giant companies such as SAS, HP, Microsoft, IBM, and Dell have already integrated Big Data in their menu. These companies are now offering total solutions. But smaller businesses rarely need complete solutions for their Big Data needs. In this Chapter, we will explore some technologies and categories that are currently in the market.

After paid solutions, we also have open-source technologies

that provide businesses with the chance to employ and try data science technologies. In this fast-paced setting, many open-source tools are now accessible to solve any Big Data challenge. Among the most popular open-source technologies is the Hadoop, which has played a critical role in the development and propagation of Big Data itself.

Hadoop

Hadoop was created as a response to the inadequacy of data storage and processing tools that are suitable for massive amounts of data that began to appear with the boom of the Internet. Google first developed the programming module MapReduce to cope with the data flow, which resulted from its strategy of organizing and making information available for everyone.

In response, Yahoo! Created Hadoop as an execution of MapReduce. This was launched in 2007 as an open-source tool through a licensing deal with Apache.

Eventually, Hadoop has developed into a massive operating system, which focuses on the parallel and distributed processing of massive amounts of data. Like other operating systems, Hadoop is composed of a file system that can write and share programs and return results.

Hadoop provides data-comprehensive distributed programs, which are capable of simultaneous running on massive groups of regular and commodity hardware. A Hadoop network is dependable and very scalable as it can be employed for massive datasets query.

Hadoop is programmed using Java so it can be run on any platform and can be used by most distributors and vendors of Big Data that have constructed layers on top of Hadoop.

The core component of Hadoop is the HDFS or Hadoop Distributed File System which can break down the data it processes into smaller files known as blocks. These data blocks are then disseminated via a cluster, which allows the map-and-reduce functions to be performed on smaller subsets rather than one large dataset.

This could increase efficiency, decrease processing time, and allows the required scalability for processing of massive amounts of data.

Meanwhile, MapReduce is a software framework, which

could process and return the massive amounts of data stored in parallel on the Hadoop network. The libraries on MapReduce are written in different programming languages and employ two steps to coordinate with unstructured and structured data.

The first step is the Map-phase that splits the data into smaller subsets, which are disseminated over the various nodes in a cluster. The nodes inside the system could perform this again, which results to a multiple level tree model, which splits the data into further smaller subsets.

With these nodes, the processed data, as well as the answer, is passed back the master node. The second step is known as the Reduce Phase, during which the master node can collect all the retrieved data and integrated it into some type of output, which can be used again. The MapReduce model manages all the different tasks in parallel and across the system. This forms the core of Hadoop.

With these integrated technologies, vast volumes of data could easily be stored, processed, and analyzed in split seconds. When an upper layer like Cloudera or Horton-works are added to this, business organizations can take advantage of real-time analytics. Hadoop offers many benefits and makes it possible to understand Big Data.

Even though MapReduce, HDFS, and Hadoop provide numerous benefits to businesses like linear scaling on commodity hardware and a high level of flaw tolerance, this is not the Holy Grail of Big Data as expected. Hadoop also has its flaws.

It is a challenge to make Hadoop operational, you should employ specialist-engineers to manage it, cluster management is not easy, and debugging really takes time and patience. Your business will definitely need specially trained IT professionals to use a complete Hadoop cluster.

Adding a Hadoop cluster in your company could be a daunting initiative and so companies, and specifically smaller companies must think cautiously whether to try it. This is another concern as more Big Data startups are now offering similar solutions, which eliminates the need to create and own the Hadoop environment. Instead, your business may just avail of Hadoop in a cloud.

Open-Source Tools

While Hadoop is the best open-source tool for Big Data, there are other open-source tools you might still consider for your business. Many of these tools offer plug-and-play scripts, drag-and-drop access, and comprehensive visualizations.

These open source tools have proven to be cost-effective and efficient in data storage, analysis, and visualization. They are now safer than they used to be, hence many companies are using them.

Among the benefits of open-source tools for Big Data are the following:

- The community around Big Data open source tools is large and active, so the products are developed and enhanced easily versus closed tools, which tend to have a longer time in the market. This also helps in encountering issues and already offers resolutions. This prevents organizations from the need to reinvent the wheel.

- Open-source tools are developed in a manner that they are running on commodity hardware, which makes it unnecessary to buy expensive equipment

- Open-source tools don't require a large investment to begin with. You just need to download it and begin working. This is a good way to try a Big Data product and know if you need it for your organization

- Open-source tools are supported with a scalable and flexible framework, which is cost-effective in managing vast quantities of data. This is highly recommended for SMEs.

The importance of open-source tools is also signified by the fact that more and more distributors and vendors who conventionally depended on proprietary platforms are now using this technology. For instance, in 2012, VMware released a new open-source project known as Serengeti, which is built to allow Hadoop run alongside the vSphere cloud built by the company.

Open-source tools also have their flaws. Primarily, open-source tools that are for free usually does not offer customer support; you might need to buy or subscribe to the premium version to receive this service. While an open-source tool could be beneficial in experimenting with new tools, it normally does not need trained It professionals who understand the open-source tool.

The biggest risk is that the developers of open-source tools may choose to discontinue developing the tools or may move to other companies. This may lead to outdated software that may not be suited for future challenges in Big Data.

Hence, the decision to employ an open-source tool should be made cautiously. Business organizations must consider not only the affordability of open source tools, but also have a comprehensive understanding of the advantages and disadvantages of the various open-source tools as compared with enterprise technology for Big Data.

13 - Tools and Analysis

Numerous enterprise Big Data technologies have been created by startups that have discovered some ways to manage massive volumes of data. They have created breakthrough technologies, which organizations can use to gain valuable data and convert into information and then into business wisdom.

Big players in the IT world have also built significant Big Data solutions in recent years, specifically, large companies that like all-inclusive Big Data solution. Moreover, many different forms of analysis could be performed employing these technologies, and every type can provide different results.

As there are Big Data solutions for almost each need and any use in any type of business, we cannot cover them all in this book. Hence, our focus will be on some the most significant areas.

Remember, one flaw of Hadoop is that it only works in groups and so it cannot easily manage massive amounts of data in real-time. But real-time streaming and data processing provides numerous advantages for business organizations.

Some technology vendors in Big Data have developed a layer on top of Hadoop or have completely developed totally fresh tools, which could cope with real-time data storage, processing, analyzing, and visualizing. These tools can now analyze structured and unstructured data in real-time, considerably enhancing the function of MapReduce and Hadoop.

Some of these technologies can combine data from various sources directly in a platform. Hence, they prevent the need for more data warehousing, but can still deliver real-time interactive charts, which are easy to control and make sense of.

Some vendors are now concentrating on delivering the final visual representation of Big Data. Visualizing structured and unstructured data is needed to convert data into information, which can be challenging. However, new Big Data companies seem to understand the importance of data visualization and have created different solutions suited for organizations.

Most visualizations are designed to appeal to the human eyes that improve the capacity of our brain to detect patterns. This strategy makes the data easy to read and understand. Using different colors and graphics will allow the audience to easily detect patterns and recognize anomalies.

Another form of data visualization is a strategy known as topological analysis that concentrates on the shape of data and could recognize clusters and statistical significance. Data professionals usually use this to discover natural patterns in clusters. This form of analysis is best visualized with three-dimensional clusters, which show the topological spaces and could be interactively explored.

It is certainly not always important to have innovative, complex, and interactive visual representations. Infographics are visual representations of data, information, or knowledge, which could help complex and difficult material easier to digest. Dashboards integrating various data streams showing conventional graphs (bar, pie, line, or column) could also offer valuable insights.

There are instances that real-time updated basic graphs showing the status of processes could actually offer more valuable insights to aid in decision making than more innovative and complex visualizations. On handheld devices, visualizations could be interpreted in a new context when a user can play interactively with the data while pinching, zooming, swiping, or rotating.

Even though the ability to visually represent real-time analytics in an attractive manner can be helpful, it is even more important for business organizations to be able to project future results.

This is largely different from current business intelligence that normally looks at what has already occurred using analytical tools that may not help you predict the future. Predictive analytics can help organizations to consider actionable intelligence according to the same data.

Hence, numerous Big Data startups are focusing on predictive modeling abilities, which will enable companies to be ready on what may come. Gathering as much data as possible while a potential customer is visiting an online store can provide valuable information.

Insights such as pages browse, and products viewed, transactional information or session insights could be integrated with historical and comprehensive customer information about past purchases and loyalty program files.

This offers a whole picture about the visitor and could help in projecting the probability of the visitor to become a paying customer. With these insights, businesses can take necessary actions.

Predictive analysis is often used in e-commerce to aid customers purchase electronics, buy airline tickets, or reserve hotel rooms. These services could aid customers buy products at the right price and at the right moment by notifying customers when prices are about to drop or what the best day of the week to shop.

In any industry, predictive analysis can be of great use, but it can be a keystone online strategy for insurance companies. This type of analytics can be used to identify which policy-holders are more likely to file claims and to estimate the risk the organization is facing. Predictive analysis works better with more data collection, because the algorithm may consider more variables for its projections.

Targeting potential customers is easier through profiling. The ultimate objective is to build a complete view of every customer so that a specific segment of once could be developed. Behavioral analysis could be used to determine patterns in structured and unstructured data across customer journeys. This will provide the organizations the ability to better understand their customers.

Customer patterns sourced from data like geographic, economic, demographic, and psychographic, can help companies to better understand their target market. Marketing and sales data like operations insights, campaign data, and conversion information, will also provide companies with precise information about their customers, which could be used to increase customer acquisitions and retention, increase cross-selling and upselling, and improve online conversion.

Customer profiles could also be employed in networks that make recommendations, which are quite common in Big Data. The most popular application for recommendation is the engine used by Amazon that allows users to receive personalized homepage when they are visiting the online store.

But retail is not the only industry that can use recommendation network to encourage customers to purchase more products. Recommendation networks are also applicable in other industries and they have different applications.

Recommendation networks are often based on two various types of algorithms, which are usually integrated. The first analyzes massive amounts of data about past purchases or choices of customers and utilizes this data for product suggestions. This is known as collaborative filtering, which is a system to recommend other products according to what other users who have the same profile have purchased.

or instance, a customer purchased W, X, Y and Z and another customer purchased V, W, X, Y, and Z. The engine will suggest product V to the first consumer because they have similar purchasing patterns. The second strategy is based on content filtering, wherein the engine utilizes a comprehensive profile of what a user has purchased in the past sessions, searched for, liked, blogged about, tweeted, websites visited, and much more.

Relying on this insight, a profile could be generated and products are suggested that can best fit this profile according to certain product attributes.

Many customers are familiar with recommendation systems from online stores, but they can also be used for B2B businesses, for instance, to suggest possible prospects to sales team. Public data sets like credit bureau profiles could be integrated with an organization's own sales and customer database to look for new relationships that a salesperson might have overlooked.

Hence, recommendation engines are becoming more common in insurance and finance companies, where they are used to recommend, on top of many benefits, sales strategies, or investment opportunities.

As a matter of fact, recommendation networks could be used anywhere consumers are searching for products or services or people. For instance, LinkedIn is now using recommendations to recommend groups, jobs, or people you may want to connect with. This suggestion function combines collaborative and content-based filtering and employs graph-based and algorithmic approach for suggestions.

Developing a digital profile of every group and identifying the most representative features of this group's members builds recommendations. LinkedIn suggests jobs by integrating various profile features like location, behavior, and attributes of connections that are similar to yours.

If you have already noticed, recommendations have now become a regular feature for many large websites, from e-commerce stores to travel pages. For any business working with suggestions, the technique is to provide relevant suggestions. This can enhance the customer experience and improve the conversion rate.

With the growing volume of data, recommendation networks will only be developed in the future. For businesses, this could mean improved targeting of products to the right individual and so, possibly an increase in the conversion rate. For customers, this will help them to easily find products that they are searching for. But this can also have a disadvantage.

If the recommendation network becomes so good and suggests services or products before consumers are even aware of them, how will this affect the possibility of a user discovering products that they are not really interested? Businesses must be aware of this, as there is a possibility that this could backfire.

The recommendations will improve if websites start using machine-learning engines for real-time suggestions because the engine will learn from recommendations that are not successful. The numerous social networks today can also create a vast amount of data about customers. Likes, Tweets, check-ins, blog posts, and comments can provide organizations answers to crucial questions like:

- What is the sentiment of my customers about my brand?

- What is the perception of my customers to my new product line?

- How can products or services be further improved for customer satisfaction?

Businesses that are using natural language processing and deep machine engines can easily interpret the meaning of comments on social media networks and add generic statements into the right mix. Social media analytics could help businesses to better understand their customers.

Once combined with other tools like usage logs, support tickets, surveys, sales data, and other sources of customer intelligence, social media analytics could convert customer retention into a data-oriented process, which will improve conversion and reduce attrition.

Segmentation and clustering analysis is a data-focused strategy to search for patterns within vast volumes of data and to cluster data sets that are alike. This goes much beyond the human-generated segments that are usually based on traits that are easy to identify like gender, age, and location.

Big Data segmentation and clustering performed by algorithms could look for patterns and segments that will otherwise stay concealed. In using self-learning engines, the segmentation will be enhanced. On the other hand, segmentation will allow the engine to learn more about the segmentation it generates.

For example, it could generate with clusters of customers who are about to become parents in a certain location in a specific type of job, and in a specific age group. The result could be used to push targeted and personalized marketing campaigns. Whatever could be discovered in the Big Data could be converted into a segment, and this could help businesses to better improve their products or services.

Outliers could be shown where clusters could be discovered. By looking for the outlier within Big Data and determining the special exception, a business could discover unexpected insights. Even though looking for an outlier can be extremely challenging, it can be easier with the use of algorithms. These abnormalities could have excellent value if they are discovered.

One example is detecting fraud or determining criminal activities in electronic banking. With self-learning algorithms and machine learning, detecting an outlier could search for correlations that are not easy to understand for humans because of the vast volumes of data needed for identifying the pattern.

In similarity search, an algorithm will try to look for an object, which is most similar to the object of interest. A good example of this is the application Shazam that can look for a song in a database containing around 12 million songs after only listening for several seconds.

Just a few years ago, SQL queries are done to search for the components that are matching specific conditions like "search all Toyota cars for sale in Kansas City". Because these algorithms are using Big Data to look for similarities, there is a high probability to succeed in finding what you are specifically looking for.

More often than not, algorithms could also run thousands of searches simultaneously in a few seconds, thereby getting results immediately.

There are now Big Data companies that are concentrating on the aspect of human capital. Based on a report from McKinsey, about 190,000 data scientists will be needed in the United States by year 2018. If Big Data can be made easier to control and organize, this concern could be addressed by eliminating the need for expensive hires.

Exploring and accessing heterogeneous data could be made so basic that users can be able to integrate Big Data sources that are stored, for instance, on Hadoop on conventional sources and do analyses on them without the need to be a specialist in data science.

There are tools that are already available in the market designed for small and medium enterprises who are interested to try Big Data strategy without spending too much, especially on hiring specialists and buying IT equipment.

The tools provide these organizations with one platform, which incorporate data from any source in any setting and allows them to perform analyses or build integrated data views. But the problem is that it can be a challenge to adapt the solution to personal needs. For comprehensive Big Data solutions, engineers and scientists will always be indispensable.

14 - Big Data for Business Organizations

According to a study conducted by Tata Consulting Services, around 47 % of the 1,217 organizations surveyed have no complete understanding of the importance of Big Data. Despite its growing popularity and breakthrough tools and technologies, only a few organizations have a deep understanding of Big Data.

Big Data provides a lot of opportunities, especially for business organizations. Based on a study published by the IBM in 2010, companies who are leveraging Big Data managed to get ahead of their competitors by 20% or up. McKinsey also reported about 60% increase in operating margins among companies who are incorporating Big Data into their business strategy.

Even though many organizations are still not embracing Big Data, it is still pouring into all industries. Even SMEs can now easily gather terabytes of data, while start-up companies can reach gigabytes without too much strain.

Global companies can generate petabytes of data easily. But simply collecting vast volumes of data is not enough to convert an organization into an information-focused organization, which could stay ahead of the game.

Take note that we are calling these organizations as information-focused organizations and not data-focused organizations. There is a subtle difference, but in fact, there are some major differences. After all, raw data is just a mess of files, and virtually useless without the right tools and the right framework in use.

Only when data is converted into information can it be beneficial for the organization. Information-focused organizations usually have a culture that depends on data that is effectively managed and used for the company's strategic decision making.

Therefore, a prerequirement for an information-focused organization is a cultural change, which will allow data and the tools needed for sound analysis and effective visualization, so the information will be available for the whole company. This will make sure that the decision will not be based on raw estimates or gut feeling.

Shifting from a culture wherein raw estimates or gut-feeling decisions are acceptable to a culture, which really integrated Big Data can be a real challenge.

So, what are the preconditions in moving from a product-focused organization to an information-focused company, in which the decisions have relied on comprehensive analysis and hard data? Where do you begin? How can you persuade the leaders of your organization to start embracing Big Data?

Many business organizations are already trying Big Data strategies. For example, Walmart local stores are permitted to change their product offerings to keep up with what local customers want to see on the shelves.

Core Traits of Information-Focused Organizations

Remember, data alone is pointless and worthless. It only gains value via comprehensive analysis using the right algorithms to retrieve the information needed in sound decision making. Organizations with a successful Big Data strategy have an information-focused culture, in which all people are completely aware that well-analyzed and visualized information could lead to better decisions.

Information can be accessed by anyone depending of course on their roles and responsibilities in the organizations. The company US Xpress is gradually becoming an information-focused organization.

Their truck drivers, for example, are equipped with iPads that they are using to access all information they need to complete their tasks. The whole organization now relies on the use of verified information in making the right decisions.

Information-focused organizations are also capable of staying ahead of the game via innovation that allows them to continuously evolve because they are early adopters of new tools and technologies and they are more likely to innovate.

Initiating Big Data strategy early on in your organization requires timing as in the next five to 10 years, it will become a common element in every form of business. It may never be even specified as Big Data but will be referred to as data again.

Another significant trait of Big Data businesses is that they gather information about anything they can find - sensor data, log data, social media data, and much more.

The strategy is to store any data you can find so you can analyze it later if the collected data can be converted into something valuable. The organization can always take a closer look if it wants to leave the data for analysis. Take note that you can't analyze a data that you don't have.

The cost of storing data should not be a hindrance, as with Hadoop you can employ commodity hardware to keep structured and unstructured data in raw form. Compressing data could even save you a lot of space. You can keep the data in a central hub to avoid balkanized IT infrastructure.

Data can be useless if they are stored in silos across the organization as it cannot be integrated easily in real time with other datasets. It will take time and effort to access and does not even provide the business a general overview of what data is available.

Certainly, information-focused organizations are gathering a lot of data - and numerous forms of data. Aside from the usual data streams like social media, websites, CRM, and logs, these businesses make certain that most of their product offerings can also gather data.

This is easier when it comes to e-commerce, but offline products can also be designed for data collection. For example, car companies can also include sensors in their cars to keep track of their car's performance and plan ahead for maintenance service to avoid breakdown.

And of course, we have already cited John Deere that adds sensors to its tractors to keep track of their performance as well as the crop and ground components. The higher the volume of data collected, the better the strategy could work. This requires creative and critical thinking to search for data in new products.

Remember, it is not even possible to convert a regular mug to a data collection material. Hence, you should think creatively when you are looking for data within the business.

Data analysis could be a challenging task when you have terabytes of data in various forms. Even though many Big Data startups are claiming that their products do not need costly IT set up, businesses executing a Big Data strategy must at least allow their IT to train on managing Big Data and run at least basic analysis.

Of course, bigger companies must concentrate on hiring Big Data specialists. For example, LinkedIn employs more than 100 data scientists.

Likewise, most of the 10,000 in-house IT personnel within General Motors have the capacity to perform analysis for Big Data. A well-trained data specialist could help the business determine the right questions you have to ask in order to gain the best answers so you can leverage on the available data.

15 - Big Data and ROI

Embracing the fact that Big Data can provide a great deal of value is a crucial starting point. But like in any business organization, Big Data, similar to any form of investment should be pitched into the executives so it could be implemented. Like in any form of new business technology, management must understand what will be the return on investment or ROI.

Big Data can affect the business in unexpected ways, and this will surely cost a lot of money to execute. How could a business determine the ROI and how much budget should be set aside for developing Big Data strategy? According to a research published by the Columbia Business School in 2012, around 57% of marketing budgets are based on past spending and not actually on the ROI.

Of course, results of previous marketing campaigns do not guarantee success. Hence, there is no point in using past budgets to identify the investment for the future. Moreover, previous fund allocations for Big Data may not even exist in your company.

The primary expense involved in setting up a Big Data

strategy is the operation and general management of Big Data into the business. Skilled Big Data personnel are also expensive, because they are rare, and dealing with thousands of nodes inside a data grid calls for special skills.

Fortunately, there are now startups specializing on Big Data strategies that can help businesses to develop cost-efficient algorithms as well as data platform solutions. Many have a flexible pricing plan, which provides some insights into the estimated cost of setting up Big Data for your organization.

But identifying the ROI is still a challenge, especially with the fact that there are no established ROI models that could be used. Conventional IT ROI frameworks are based on traditional factors such as minimizing data center equipment, data center energy savings plan, or speed per transaction.

Normally, what could be expected from the data analytics remain totally unknown until it is completed, which makes the conventional models unusable.

In order to develop ROI for Big Data, organizations should begin with the following pointers:

1. Specify your goals in using Big Data, and then estab-

lish your expected results. For instance, your goal might be to better understand your customers that will provide you the insights to decide on what you can do to provide better customer service and experience. As a matter of fact, 86% of people are keener to pay more if they experience better customer service. Choosing the right goals could, therefore, aid in identifying ROI.

2. Choose the tools required to meet your goals. Different Big Data startups provide various solutions at the various price ranges. You can use open-source tools but you can also use premium tools to help you in executing your plan. Based on the tools you want to use, commodity hardware or a cloud solution may be required. This will provide you more insights on what will be the involved costs.

3. Begin with a pilot project that will help you achieve your goals on a smaller scale. The investments required are usually less problematic for finance executives to make available. The returns and costs will provide far more important information into the ROI compared to the benchmarks or pre-Big Data figures.

If done properly, Big Data can provide more value to your business. Value could be in the manner of faster time in delivering product to the market because you know precisely what customers like as well as their purchasing behavior. Big Data could also help you to learn about your competitors and gain a deeper insight of the possible market movement.

Big Data can also provide efficient management of your resources. Your ROI will depend on the goals set, the size of the business, the tools that were chosen, the hardware available, and the processes that are executed. Many factors are affecting the ROI for Big Data. When selected with caution, Big Data could lead to a positive ROI and setting up a pilot project could provide you the important insights you need.

16 - Big Data Financials

In a conventional sense, IT is seen by businesses as a way to save money. Big Data, on the other hand, is positioned as a way to create value and so bring money to the organization. Hence, it has a place to your balance sheets.

According to a study conducted by SAS and published in 2012, about 20% of big companies in the UK are already assigning the monetary value to their data as appeared on their balance sheets. It is becoming clear that more and more companies are starting to understand the value of data.

It is crucial for organizations to determine how they should proceed with Big Data, and how they should account for it on their financials.

As you already know of course, a balance sheet will tell you the financial health of an organization at a specific period of time. This includes the assets and liabilities of the company.

Assets could be tangible such as (hardware, land, or machines) or intangible (copyrights, algorithms, trademarks), On the other hand, liabilities are legal obligations or debts that arise during the business operations such as accounts payable and loans.

Data could be classified as an intangible asset. As a matter of fact, in 2011, AT&T has valued data such as customer database at $2.7 billion. If this type of data could be included, surely the derived value of data such as information or insights from Big Data could be classified as an asset.

But Data could also become a liability if not managed well. One example is the case of Diginotar, a data security firm in Netherlands, which went bankrupt because its data was not properly secured.

Its data hubs were hacked and the data it supposed to be protecting for its clients were compromised. This shows that Big Data is a critical element, and could be turned into a liability instead of an asset if not protected properly.

Let's say that Big Data is an asset for an organization, and it must appear on the business balance sheet as an important metric to determine the value of business.

If this is the case, then it is also important to identify the value of Big Data as it is being used within the business. Identifying the cost of Big Data seems a bit easier. All you have to do is to get the sum of how much it costs to build, maintain, update, keep, retrieve, archive, visualize, access, and get rid of data. But identifying the ROI on Big Data initiatives is a real challenge, because of specific uncertainties.

That is why you can use the phrase Return on Data or ROD as a metric to identify the value of Big Data for your business. Better data usage could result in more insights about your customers, which can lead to improved products delivered in a shorter period of time that can eventually lead to a spike in Customer Lifetime Value (CLV).

The distinction between the projected CLV and the present CLV can be the Big Data value. If the purpose of Big Data strategy for a business is to reduce waiting time for airline companies, the ROD can be the number of hours saved annually less than the costs needed to establish Big Data.

Adding Big Data on the balance sheet of a business organization is a major decision that must be well founded. A positive point of adding Big Data on your balance sheet is that it will boost better control and supervision of the data.

Adding it on the balance sheet would make people understand the value of data for the business. This may lead to better use of it and can encourage acceptance of Big Data as part of the organizational strategy.

17 - Big Data for Small and Medium Enterprises

There is a misconception that Big Data is only for the big boys; and the small players are not capable enough to join the movement. Even SMEs who have limited budgets and capable enough of gathering small amounts of data could still develop their own Big Data strategies and evolve as an information-focused organization.

Take note that even SMEs also have their own distributors and suppliers. When these organizations begin to collaborate with each other and decide to share their data, the volume of accessible data can expand.

This process is also being practiced by large companies. For instance, Nike is now sharing data from all its suppliers, which allows other players in the supply chain to access the database for their decision making.

When SMEs begin to use and integrate data from their vendors and suppliers, they will have enough data to analyze and visualize and guide them for making better decisions. Another option is to integrate their current small data with public datasets, which are becoming available.

In addition, more and more public platforms are becoming available for SMEs to download or purchase more datasets. Another advantage is that integrating current data with new public datasets could totally generate new results like discovering new target market or groups.

It is not ideal for SMEs to look at the data that they have already collected. Instead, it should embrace new ways of collecting data. Creativity is crucial in this area, as in the end, any product or service could be converted into the data if used with sensors.

Sensors are becoming more affordable each day, and integrating sensors into current products could totally deliver new data sets that could provide unexpected insights.

Take note that Big Data is not all about velocity or volume. It also touches variety. The real power of Big Data is the capacity to integrate structured and unstructured datasets to gain new insights. Unstructured data are sourced out from different places such as emails, files, visuals, social data, and even audio files.

Integrating several minor data sets could provide similar insights as integrating large datasets. Gigabytes of data could, therefore, offer SMEs with the same insights as exabytes or petabytes do for big players.

In order to start using Big Data, SMEs should be flexible and agile. They should look for solutions that can match their needs as well as resources. Rather than building a complete Big Data solution from HP, SAS, or IBM, SMEs can instead use cloud solutions developed by smaller, and so more agile startups.

Moreover, they can also develop their own Big Data solution using open-source tools. Even though this will require specialists, it is still more affordable. Open source tools are free to use unless you want to try the premium services and the needed equipment and technologies are getting more affordable these days.

It is certain that Big Data is not only for big companies. There is an abundance of opportunities for SMEs to gain important insights from the current datasets. However, SMEs should be more creative in setting up their Big Data solutions.

They should think critically and creatively to see the opportunities for Big Data inside and outside the business. This is also necessary for big players if they are interested to take full benefit of Big Data.

Hence, small data could become Big Data by creatively integrating different datasets with various forms of data. For instance, you can integrate weather data with an ice cream store's sales data to find the effect of rain on items sold and so change your purchasing plan. Integrate your customer data with an online sentiment to delight them and nurture the relationships.

Monitor how your customers behave through your store and integrate it with your sales data to see how you could adjust and develop profiles to see how you could optimize your multichannel strategy for your smaller retail stores. There are endless opportunities and small data also has the power to gain the business important insights with the right tools and strategy.

18 - Security and Ethics

Big Data caused the development of breakthrough technologies and tools, which usually come along with concerns. With Big Data, these issues include security as well as ethics. As we gear towards collecting more data, regulations are also needed to make sure that these concerns are addressed.

In 2013, Edward Snowden leaked out the PRISM, which revealed that privacy can be compromised with the emergence of Big Data solutions. In the US, the NSA used the PRISM for raw intelligence for its reports. The agency has direct access to information on the servers of important sites including Facebook, Apple, and Google.

Furthermore, Snowden proved that the US government also has access to private conversations through text from Chinese residents, which the British government used to monitor its leaders during the G20 summit in the UK in 2009. This involves about 39,000 terabytes of data every day. The PRISM leak made the public aware of the possible danger of Big Data on compromising individual privacy.

Regardless of the benefits of Big Data for organizations, the issue of privacy cannot be ignored when collecting information. It is crucial to look ahead their privacy concerns and make certain that these are addressed to avoid problems later on. In essence, Big Data is not a pro-privacy innovation, as even concealed data can still be traced back to its sources as long as sufficient data is available.

Closely associated to privacy is the ethical concern on Big Data. Almost everyone is now creating data using different forms of devices, applications, or products. It is crucial to discuss who owns the data created and what they are doing with the data they collect.

More often than not, customers don't have the slightest idea of what companies are doing with their data, which could have negative consequences not only for the customers but also for the business as well.

Because of the quantified-self movement, many applications (most are free) are now gathering a lot of data about people. About 60% of Americans today are using a form of app to monitor their exercise, weight, or diet. But in a sense, using these apps are not for free. Using "free" products or services are being paid by your personal data. For most customers, it is not certain where the data goes.

Most services that people are using today started as free and friendly. People think it is fine, and still fine, to use services such as Facebook or Google or other online applications that are now very popular.

People are so used to this concept that everything that is online can be used for free, which they now find it impossible to pay for premium services. They are so hooked into these services that they cannot let go of them in spite of the possible privacy concerns.

But only a few years ago, businesses have slowly yet surely embraced the storage and usage of more data in profiling consumers, while continuously adding free services.

Hence, organizations that people thought were linking them to their friends and offering information as a free commodity are now using them for targeted advertisements using data generated about them from these very organizations.

It is still not fully known what the effect on this on ethics or privacy is. People are becoming more aware of the problem. The result is an initiative in which users choose to pay for the service rather than data. One example is App.net where users are paying a premium fee to use the platform without the ads.

Each click, each black filled out, every piece of information on how usually customers are using a product or service, how they use it when they use it could get converted into data-focused product enhancements or can be used to serve targeted ads. Because services are becoming more costly to build or maintain, the advertisement becomes bigger.

Of course, investors will expect a return on their investments, especially with public organizations. A great example of this is no less than Facebook, where the ad space on the news feed is becoming more important.

As long as Facebook users don't think that this is compromising their privacy, the social media giant will continue to show more ads. Its graph search is using more information from its users and purchases information from data suppliers to enhance its targeted ads.

This is a valid and legal business model, which is being used by many organizations for many years. As users are becoming more aware of this and has also raised questions about it, there is also the need for organizations to educate their users on how their private data is used. People have to be more cautious about their online activities.

People must really begin to think of every data point as an economic process between the service provider and the user, and organizations should also encourage transparency. They have to be more careful and encourage people to read the fine print before agreeing to the terms and conditions. They must also check their privacy settings on social media sites.

More and more websites are also now educating their users on how they can adjust their privacy settings. But still, many organizations are not making it easy for people to understand how they are using data. You may think that posting your privacy policy online is enough.

However, many users are still not fully aware of the real essence of a privacy policy. Organizations must not only provide information to their consumers, but they should also try to protect their data from intruders.

Hence, organizations must be very clear about what data is

gathered and what are they doing with it. Transparency should also be a major concern for organizations who want to work with Big Data. Also, they should also provide users the chance to use their service without collecting or storing any data. In this case, the user may pay for premium service instead.

19 - The Future of Data Science

Web 3.0, also known as the semantic web is usually regarded as the next stage of the Internet. Pushed by the World Wide Web Consortium or W3C, the goal is to shift the existing web of semi-structured and unstructured data into a web of data. W3C believes that this will enable everyone to easily share and access data across conventional boundaries of enterprise and community.

Basically, Web 3.0 will allow people and devices (read: IoT) to be connected with each other and share and reuse data in various forms across various applications and organizations in real time. Big Data plays a core role in this development.

All Big Data technologies that are being developed such as open-source tools, Hadoop, and the technology being created by startups, will boost the evolution to Web 3.0. Its evolution requires that linking, analyzing, and processing data become less expensive and more functional.

One good example of the semantic web is Google's Knowledge Graph, which was released in 2012. The search engine giant refers to this as the future of search, because it is not indexing strings but rather things.

Google has managed to contain more than 18 billion facts about connections between various objects that are built to understand the context of keywords for search purposes. The mission is to enable the search engine so users can just ask computers natural questions.

Organizations who want to be involved with Big Data should not only be ready for the development of Web 3.0, it should also prepare its organization to take full advantage of the benefits of Big Data. Once the semantic web becomes functional, Big Data's future, could really make waves in many industries, and will start the era of convergence between data, networks, and computing.

The future of Big Data will allow people to ask questions and look for answers more easily by using natural conversations. At present, users have to know what they need to know, but eventually, this will be about the things that we may still not aware that we want to know.

Eventually, Big Data becomes so well advanced that organizations will already have the answers before they even ask the questions. Advanced categorization and pattern detection will allow algorithms to guide organizations in making decisions. Comprehensive and attractive visualizations will also become more essential and could help organizations make sense of vast volumes of data.

The future of Big Data will also change how we analyze the brontobytes of data. In the past, we tried to understand the organizations or the surrounding environment by analyzing the data available through descriptive analysis.

Through Big Data, we have entered into a new age of predictive analysis, wherein we can find answers to try predict the future. This attempts to provide a recommendation for important decisions according to possible results in the future.

Predictive analysis can provide your organization with actionable insights according on data. This offers an estimation about the possibility of a future result. In order to do this, different strategies can be used, which includes game theory, modeling, data mining, and machine learning. Predictive analysis can also help in identifying future opportunities as well as risks.

Transactional and historical data are used to detect patterns, while algorithms and statistical data are used to find the relationships in different datasets.

Predictive analysis plays a critical role in the Big Data era, and there are numerous tools and technologies that organizations can use to make a highly educated guess on what could happen in the future. With predictive analysis, it is crucial to gather as much as data as possible to improve the quality of predictions.

20 - The Era of Brontobytes

In the coming years, Big Data scientists will be in extremely high demand, but the actual winners in this field are the companies allows Big Data to be easy to use, execute, and understand that hiring data scientists becomes unnecessary.

Big companies will always get the services of Big Data Scientists but SMEs, which compose a large market when combined, will not be able to afford hiring specialists. Startups offering Big Data solutions for SMEs to the point of ignoring the need of hiring data scientists will definitely gain a high advantage in the field.

The algorithms developed by these Big Data startups will even become smarter, smartphones will become more sophisticated yet easier to use, and people will be able to use handheld devices with enough computing power to easily visualize data in real-time. Furthermore, with the IoT and the billions of sensors, the volumes of data that requires processing will exponentially expand.

The future of Big Data is certain. It will become bigger and bigger, and the brontobytes of tomorrow will become the terabytes of today. Data storage will become widely access-ible and more affordable. Referring to brontobytes of data as Big Data will eventually come off, and Big Data will be referred to as just data.

But before going that phase, the increasing volume of data that is processed by organizations will also create privacy and ethical concerns. Organizations who will protect privacy and adhere to ethical standards will not only survive but will also stay ahead of the game.

21 - Conclusion

Thanks again for taking the time to buy this book!

You should now have a good understanding of Big Data, and be able to use the practical information you have learned in this book to steer your business in the right direction.

Book 4 - Cryptocurrency

A Beginner's Guide To Understanding And Winning With Fintech (Bitcoin, Blockchain, Trading, Investing, Mining, Digital Money, Smart Contracts)

1 - Introduction

Thank you for taking the time to buy this book. This book will serve as your guide in exploring the exciting opportunities and risks in the world of cryptocurrencies. Learning is crucial if you want to succeed in any endeavor, and this is true when it comes to cryptocurrencies, which is regarded as the future cash of the world.

Through this book, you will be able to learn the following:

- The origins of cryptocurrencies and why it is now becoming popular among non-technical users

- The Blockchain technology and why it is considered as a breakthrough innovation in the world of financial technology

- The pros and cons of using digital currencies

- The top cryptocurrencies according to popularity, value, and market capitalization

- How you can make money in cryptocurrency

- The future outlook of cryptocurrency – Is it a fad or a breakthrough technology?

1 - INTRODUCTION

Once again, thanks for buying this book, I hope you find it to be helpful!

2 - What Is Cryptocurrency

A cryptocurrency is a currency in virtual or digital form, which utilizes cryptographic technology to add security to process transfer and safekeeping. Because of this security feature, a cryptocurrency can be difficult to counterfeit.

Its organic nature is a distinctive feature of a cryptocurrency and usually regarded as its best feature. No central authority releases cryptocurrency, so in theory, it cannot be subjected to government manipulation or interference.

Early Days of Cryptocurrency

Although Bitcoin, arguably the most popular cryptocurrency today, was only introduced in 2008, the first recorded attempt in using a virtual form of cash was during the late 1980s. In the Netherlands, gas stations in the rural areas were often robbed. Obviously, the owners were not happy with the circumstances as they need to operate day and night so lorries can refuel.

One suggested the idea of loading money into smart cards, which was then being tested out. It was the beginning of electronic cash. Truck drivers were provided with these cards instead of cash, and so the incidence of robbery went down.

During the same time, Albert Heijn (a major retailer in Netherlands) was lobbying for banks to come up with a system that will allow consumers to directly pay from their bank accounts, which later developed as Point of Sale or POS.

Virtual Cash

Meanwhile in the US, a Cryptographer David Chaum had been working on a system that will use virtual cash. His research on currency and privacy caused him to believe that to be able to do business safely, there is a need for a currency that will mimic the purpose of actual bank notes and coins.

In particular, Chaum is looking into the capacity of a system that will allow anyone to pay safely and privately without the interference of a third party such as a bank.

David Chaum created an extension of the RSA algorithm, which is now being used in encrypting data in the web. This blinding formula enables anyone to transfer a number to anyone, and this number is subject to modification by the receiver. Once the receiver keeps the coin into the bank, it still has the authentic signature of the mint. However, this is not the same number that the mint has signed.

This system allowed the coin to be changed without a trace and without damaging the original signature of the mint. Therefore, the bank or the mint is blind to the process. This interest, as well as more favorable policies on privacy, persuaded Chaum to live in Netherlands.

He worked with the CWI, which was a bastion for mathematical research and cryptography. During his tenure at CWI, he created DigiCash and led to the creation of virtual money. He mentored other cryptographers and pioneers in cryptocurrency including Bryce Wilcox-Ahearn, Nick Szabo, Marcel Van Der Peijl, Gary Howland, Niels Ferguson, and Stefan Brands.

The invention of virtual cash caused a frenzy and it has caught a lot of attention from the public. However, David Chaum and his team made some misfortunes and experienced some entanglements with the Central Bank of Netherlands or the DNB.

It turned out that Chaum agreed that the virtual cash will only be offered to the banks. This arrangement then caused the company to offer the virtual cash through numerous banks, which led to the company's bankruptcy in 1998.

The feverish attention in the press attracted potential big deals such as Deutsche Bank and Microsoft, but Chaum failed to take advantage to propel. It was even reported that Microsoft offered as much as $180 million to Chaum so that every Windows PC will be enabled with DigiCash. Chaum thought the offer was not enough, and so Microsoft backed down, and Chaum went bankrupt.

Online Cash

Despite Chaum's bankruptcy, DigiCash was a breakthrough invention, and in fact, on its coattails, many startups were created to work on this area. During the 1990s, the interest in virtual cash increased in the USA primarily because Europe has implemented regulatory policies on digital cash. Meanwhile, in the US, Netscape had just launched its IPO.

However, the first wave of using cryptocurrency immediately faded and was replaced by the second wave of online cash. The first wave of excitement was First Virtual, which was the predecessor of PayPal. While First Virtual was strict on its policy of being a merchant before accepting money, PayPal allowed cash to be transferred from one person to another.

Hence, PayPal became more popular than First Virtual who acted like regular banks. PayPal also introduced some innovations such as its system of literally handing cash via the Palm Pilot, which was very popular among geeks.

This focus on geeks, was immediately abandoned as the company realized that majority of its users are really looking for a way to send and receive money through the internet. It also secured a large consumer base within the eBay community, so PayPal propelled to great heights.

This popularity has proven that online can become a protocol of choice, even for financial transactions. Hence, the ideas of Chaum were nevertheless used but largely forgotten in North America. However, Chaum's system was still thriving in Russia through the use of WebMoney. Several startups were also established to work on harnessing money through the web.

E-gold was a company that initially succeeded in this field. Its operation was based in the US, but it was registered as a corporation in the Caribbean. This company offers a very easy system - a client sends in precious metals such as gold or silver, and the company will credit e-gold to his account. The client can also purchase new e-gold by sending a wire to the company, which will buy and keep the physical gold.

The company became popular among gold traders and investors. Because the company was based in the Caribbean, there is no need for the US government to approve the process. The system enticed the American market for goldbugs as well as the increasingly global community of online traders who need to facilitate international payments.

As you might even guess, e-gold was then subjected to a government investigation, mainly because of the system's policy of allowing anyone to sign up for an account. Even though this is not illegal, the increasing incidence of online scams caught the attention of FBI.

The Feds raided the company's office in Florida, which has cracked down its operation and caused the downfall of e-gold as an online currency. Also, FBI winded up similar companies, which ensured the end of the second wave of the new currency.

Before the events of the September 11 attacks, the US was quite liberal about allowing alternative currencies. The US government saw the potential of an alternative currency for business and innovation. But after September 11, this perception dramatically changed.

Cryptocurrencies were perceived to be the platform for facilitating transactions to fund drug deals and terrorist activities. Hence, cryptocurrencies were targeted for control.

Bitcoin

Before the Nixon Shock, the US dollar has been based on the amount of gold that the US Treasury holds. Practically, you can exchange your dollars for its value in gold. In comparison, cryptocurrencies such as Bitcoin, are not based on gold or silver but based on mathematical mints.

Bitcoins are created using a sophisticated layer of mathematical formula, which runs on computers. The network has access to a public ledger through Blockchain technology which records and confirms every processed transaction.

A single entity like the central bank cannot control the Bitcoin ledger. The primary concept of Bitcoin is decentralization, which refers to the independent nature of the transaction from the interference of manipulation of a government, a country, or a bank.

But who created Bitcoin? Well, there is no clear answer to this as the popular name of the creator is still shrouded in mystery. The publisher of the whitepaper describing Bitcoin and the use of Blockchain system is just a nome de plume - Satoshi Nakamoto. His Blockchain account is no longer active, and even the BTC in his wallet was never spent.

However, some people believe that Satoshi Nakamoto refers to the group of people who are experts in cryptocurrency including Charles Bry, Vladimir Oksman, and Neal King. This group actually filed for a patent for the Bitcoin before the Bitcoin domain was purchased. This is very far from a mere coincidence.

On October 31, 2008, a whitepaper was published describing the foundation of the Bitcoin system. It was entitled "Bitcoin: A Peer-to-Peer Electronic Cash System" was published to a cryptography mailing list. The author was listed as Satoshi Nakamoto.

However, it was two months prior to this publication that the Bitcoin.org was purchased specifically on August 18, 2008. The prototype version of Bitcoin was only announced on January 8, 2009, and it began the frenzy for Bitcoin mining.

It is just fitting that the creator of Bitcoin hides its real identity, as privacy is a key concern for Bitcoin and its users. While it is still unknown who created Bitcoin, it is a fact that this breakthrough technology has started a revolution in the financial world.

3 - How Cryptocurrency Works?

As the name suggests, cryptocurrencies are currencies that are encrypted in code. As a currency, it can be transmitted from one person to another and verified in a public ledger through a mining process.

In this Chapter, we will take a general overview of how cryptocurrencies such as Bitcoin work. We first need to go over the basics of cryptocurrency, and then we will also cover the other important features of common cryptocurrencies today.

Basic Concepts of Cryptocurrency

To fully understand the mechanism behind cryptocurrencies, it is important to understand first some basic concepts: public ledgers, transactions, and mining.

Public Ledger

In cryptocurrency, a public ledger is used to store all verified transaction from the creation of a cryptocurrency. When you use a cryptocurrency, your identity will be encrypted, and the system will use other encryption techniques to make certain that the record keeping will be accurate.

The public ledger ensures that the specific digital wallet could calculate the correct available amount. In addition, new currency transactions could be verified to ensure that every transaction only uses coins that are owned by a certain identity. In Bitcoin, this public ledger is known as a Blockchain.

Transactions

Similar to a bank transaction, a transaction in cryptocurrency refers to the transmission of cryptocurrency from one owner of a digital wallet to another. This transaction is filed into the public ledger for verification.

Once there is a transaction, digital wallets use an encryption to bestow a mathematical code that the transaction originates from a specific owner of a wallet. The verification process may take a bit of time (about 10 minutes) for BTC while the network verifies the transaction and file them to the ledger.

Mining

In cryptocurrency, mining refers to the process of verifying the transaction and linking them to the public ledger. To link a transaction to the public ledger, a miner should be able to solve a mathematical problem. In Bitcoin, mining is open source, so anyone could verify any transaction. The first miner who will solve the mathematical puzzle can link a block to the ledger.

The manner in which the transactions, processes, and the ledger work together assure that no single person could easily add or modify a block. When a block is linked to the ledger, all related transactions become permanent and a minimal transaction fee will be added to the wallet of the miner alongside the newly generated coins. The mining process provides value to the coin.

How Bitcoin Works

Arguably, the most popular cryptocurrency today is Bitcoin, and to understand how Bitcoin works, we can understand how a cryptocurrency works.

3 - HOW CRYPTOCURRENCY WORKS?

The whole Bitcoin system runs on a Peer-to-Peer or P2P network, which is similar to file-sharing networks similar to the ones, which allow people to easily transfer various forms of data, which includes pictures, music, videos, and more. Basically, a P2P system is a resilient platform.

Hence, there is no central hub that runs all Bitcoin transactions. Rather, every computer of a Bitcoin user is a part of the network, which collectively shares the load of generating the digital currency and recording their transactions. This decentralized feature makes Bitcoin free from government interference.

Bitcoins should be mined first before you can use them. Any computer can start Bitcoin mining by using a free mining application. This requires the whole network of computers to perform a set of work before getting bitcoins as a reward.

In general, this work entails several computers solving mathematical problems, and the rewards will be given to the owner of the PC, which completes the calculation at hand. Hence, it is not surprising that some people have decided to invest in super powerful computers for bitcoin mining.

The specific amount of work needed is variable. The network can adjust the workload so that the number of bitcoins will increase at a stable and predetermined number. This will continue to perform until it reaches 21 million, which is the maximum number of bitcoins in circulation.

At present, the mining process could generate 25 bitcoins every 10 minutes. And every four years will be decreased by 50% until the maximum limit of Bitcoins will be achieved. This is projected to happen in the year 2140. After this, the circulation of Bitcoin will be static.

You have to keep your bitcoins in your digital wallet. If you receive or send bitcoins, they will be validated by a digital signature, which is known as an encryption key that safeguards the currency from counterfeits. The network keeps the whole transaction in a public ledger known as Blockchain, which is a safe way to monitor the circulation of bitcoins.

This is possible thanks to the open-source nature of Bitcoin. As a short background, the principle of open source software is often used by programmers who are against corporate control and profiteering.

Hence, any experienced programmer can see how the programming behind the system is working. Non-programmers may think that this is a threat to the security of the network, but this is actually an ingenious way for the whole network to confirm the legitimacy for every transfer.

Bitcoin as a Cryptocurrency

Similar to any currency, you can keep your Bitcoins in your account, and hopefully they appreciate in value. You can also cash them out and convert into your preferred traditional currency. If you choose to keep them on your computer, it is important to take note that there is no central network that will serve as a backup for your data stored in your wallet.

Therefore, you should keep your own record of bitcoins. It is recommended to keep this record on a device like a flash drive, which you can keep away in a safe location. You might lose all your record of bitcoin savings if you lose your laptop or your computer crashes down.

You can never reverse a Bitcoin transaction, and it is quite fast to complete. But because the verification process for

Bitcoin transaction requires data sharing with the whole network, there are times that you have to wait for a few minutes before you can complete payment.

Because Bitcoin is not regulated by any government, it is easy to transfer them to any point of the globe and without paying the high fees that banks usually charge for overseas transactions. And with the absence of a governing body, your Bitcoin account has no restrictions, and can never be subjected to a free order.

This sounds too good to be true, and in fact, many people are questioning the legitimacy of cryptocurrencies. It seems dubious that a currency can just appear in a few minutes online and have real value. We can discuss here the comprehensive and philosophical basis of money, but we can sum up the essence of currency with this - all currencies are valuable because people agreed to believe that they have value.

People who use Bitcoin trust the encryption and mathematics of the whole system, and this trust has been cultivated through the years, and similar to any currency, has been accepted by a large community.

Current Worth of Bitcoin

As of May 2017, 1 BTC is equivalent to $1,223, which is a significant jump from its value in 2016 when it was only about $ 770 on average. The price of Bitcoin is also dependent on the volume of mining processes, because of more mining activities, the more it becomes difficult and so more expensive to generate new coins.

Therefore, the price of Bitcoin should increase as the production cost also increases. The aggregate power of the mining network of Bitcoin has increased to threefold over the past year.

How Bitcoin Mining Works?

Bitcoin transactions happen all the time, and without a way to keep all these transactions, there is no way to monitor who has paid what. This is being taken care of the Bitcoin network by collecting all the transactions that have occurred during a specific period in the list known as the block. It is the role of the miner to verify these transactions and add them to the public ledger.

This public ledger is basically a long list of blocks called the Blockchain. This could be used to explore any transaction made between Bitcoin users and at any point in the system.

If the system creates a new block, it will be added to the chain, which creates the whole list of all the transactions that happened in the network. Because the ledger is public, everyone who participates in the network can access the transactions.

However, a general ledger should be trusted, and it should be kept in a digital format. This is an area of concern because it could be difficult to be certain that the Blockchain remains solid and untampered. This is the reason why the role of Bitcoin miners is important.

Once a block of transactions is generated, Bitcoin miners verify the process. They read the information in the block, and use a certain mathematical formula, which converts it into another code. This code is known as a hash, which is simply a random sequence of numbers and letters. This hash is kept along with the block, at the end of the Blockchain at any given time.

It can be easy to generate a hash from a group of data such as a Bitcoin block. However, it can be quite impossible to read the data just by looking at the hash. And although it can be easy to generate a hash from a large group of data, every data is one of a kind. The hash will be completely changed if you change just one character in a block.

Bitcoin miners are not just using the transactions in a block to create a hash. Other forms of data are also used, which includes the hash of the last stored block in the chain.

In a way, this becomes an electronic version of a wax seal because the hash of each block is generated using the hash of the prior block. This verifies that this block, as well as the block after it - is genuine because everyone will notice if the block has been tampered.

If a user attempts to tamper a transaction by changing a block, which has already been linked into the chain, the hash of this block will change. If one user verifies the authenticity of the block by taking a look at the hash, he will find that the hash doesn't align with the one already linked with the block. Hence, this block will be immediately flagged as tampered.

Because every hash of the block is used to help in creating the hash of the next block in the chain, changing the block will also make the next block misaligned, too. This will continue all the way down, which will throw the whole chain in a chaos.

This is how miners verify the block. They are all in a competition to perform the seal off through the help of software that is programmed particularly for block mining. Each time a user successfully generates a hash, he receives 25 Bitcoins, the system will update the block, and every participant in the network will be notified. This is the main motivation to keep mining and keep the transactions happening.

The main concern is that it can be easy to generate a hash from a data group, as computers are very powerful nowadays. As a response, the Bitcoin network should make it more difficult to do this, or else anyone will be able to hash thousands of bitcoins every minute, and the currency will be ubiquitous.

The special protocol used by Bitcoin makes it extra difficult to mine the currency by requiring proof of work.

This protocol will not accept any old hash. It requires that a has a certain block should look a specific way. It should have a specific number of zeroes at the beginning. You just can't tell what a hash will look like before you generate it, and when you introduce a new piece of data in the chain, the hash will be changed.

Miners are not allowed to interfere with the block's data transaction, but they should modify the data that they are using to generate a specific hash. This is possible by using a random piece of data known as nonce, which is used with the system to generate a hash.

When the hash does not fit the required format, the nonce will be changed, and the entire system will be hashed again. The user may take several attempts to search for a nonce that works and all the miners are performing this task simultaneously. This is how you can earn bitcoins through mining.

Getting a Bitcoin Wallet

Just like other currencies, you need to have a method to keep your cryptocurrencies. When it comes to Bitcoins, you have to have a digital wallet, which actually behaves a lot more like a bank account.

Different wallets offer different levels of security depending on the security level you prefer. Some wallets can be used like daily spending accounts and can be best compared to the actual physical wallet while other wallets are protected with military-grade encryption as they may contain Bitcoins that are worth millions of dollars.

There are three primary options when it comes to digital wallets:

- A web-based online service

- A digital wallet kept on the hard drive of your PC

- Vault service, which stores the Bitcoins or a multi-signature wallet using a number of codes to safeguard the account

Digital wallets have their vulnerabilities. When you keep a cryptocurrency locally on your hard drive, you need to ensure that you regularly backup your data so you can still access your record if your drive crashes down. Digital wallets also use different levels of degrees to security against hackers from minimal security (username and password) to maximum security (multi-factor authentication).

Cryptocurrency Transactions

There are also different types of transactions involving cryptocurrencies. Some are basic transactions such as a usual trade for online services while others involve hundreds of thousands of Bitcoins for corporate trading. Most wallets and exchanges will keep the amounts of cryptocurrency for the user, much like a conventional bank account.

4 - What Makes Cryptocurrencies Different

Even though there are certain exceptions, there are several factors that make cryptocurrencies quite different from the current financial systems:

Value

As you have already learned earlier, a currency is genuine if it has an agreed value. Any currency such as the Euro represents value because Europeans agree that a piece of special paper has value. This is the same principle followed by cryptocurrencies.

We have learned that the value of cryptocurrencies, such as Bitcoins, is created by miners, who are people who are running programs on their computers to solve mathematical problems. The work behind mining digital currencies provides them value, while the fluctuating demand and supply cause the value to fluctuate.

Again, the concept of work providing value to a currency is known as a proof of work approach, which is also known as proof of stake in other forms of digital currencies. Value is generated when transactions are linked to the public ledger as generating a confirmed block also requires work.

Pseudonymity

Cryptocurrency owners store their digital money in a protected wallet. The identification of the coin holder will be stored in an encrypted location, which they can control, but not linked to the identity of the person.

The link between the user and the digital currency is pseudonymous instead of anonymous because ledgers can be accessed by the public, and so these ledgers could be used to get more information about groups of people in the system.

Proof of Work

Many forms of cryptocurrencies today are using proof of work model, which uses a complicated calculation but easy to confirm mathematical problem to restrict the use of cryptocurrency mining. Basically, this is a complicated captcha, which needs high-level computational capacity.

Open Source

Cryptocurrencies are usually open source, which means that anyone can create APIs for free and can participate in the network.

Digital

Conventional currency is defined by an actual object to represent value (USD, EUR, JPY), but cryptocurrencies are all digital. Digital currencies are kept in digital wallets and can be transferred digitally to other wallets. For example, there is no physical object that represents Bitcoin.

Decentralized

The currencies that are in circulation are under control of a central government through its central bank, and so their production could be regulated by a third party. The creation and transaction involving cryptocurrencies are controlled by code, open source, and depends on the P2P network. No single authority could interfere in cryptocurrencies.

Cryptographic

Encryption is a primary feature of cryptocurrency. This is used to control the production of the digital currency and to confirm transactions.

Adaptive Scaling

Basically, cryptocurrencies are produced with a number of factors to make certain that they can work well regardless of the volume of transaction.

For example, Bitcoin is designed to permit for a single block transaction to be mined in 10-minute intervals. The algorithm adapts after 2016 blocks, which is about 2 weeks to make the mining more difficult or easier depending on the time that it took for the blocks to be mined.

The mining is easy if it only takes 10 days to mine the 2016 blocks. Therefore, the system will increase the difficulty. The difficulty will decrease if it takes more than 15 days to mine the 2016 blocks.

Several other measures are integrated into cryptocurrencies to permit adaptive scaling, which includes decreasing the reward for mining as more currencies are mined and creating scarcity by restricting the supply over time.

Don't worry if at this point you are still a bit confused on how cryptocurrencies work. It can be a real challenge to wrap your head around the basic concepts of cryptocurrencies. These concepts may be easy for some, while for others, may require a different way of discussion.

The technique with cryptocurrencies is not to be worried if you are not understanding them first. Every chapter in this book will help you learn more about cryptocurrencies until you develop a natural appreciation for them and eventually use them.

5 - Advantages and Disadvantages of Using Cryptocurrencies

After learning how cryptocurrencies work, it is ideal to learn more about the advantages and disadvantages of using a digital currency. There are several advantages that make cryptocurrency better than the traditional currencies today. However, this is still far from being perfect, so most cryptocurrencies also have their flaws. We will explore the pros and cons of cryptocurrencies in this chapter.

Advantages of Cryptocurrencies

More Freedom

With cryptocurrencies, it is easy to send and receive money anytime and anywhere you are. There is no need to worry about exchange rates, scheduling transfers to consider bank holidays or other restrictions we usually encounter when we transfer money. You can control your own money with cryptocurrencies as there is no central governing authority that will interfere with the transactions.

Let's take a look at one real example of how a digital currency works without interference from the government.

Today, there is a self-imposed crisis in Venezuela. There is a scarcity of goods in the country, while black markets are rampant. Money is also scarce, and some people have turned to using cryptocurrencies, primarily Bitcoin in order to survive.

The government subsidizes electricity, which has provided some people to earn income through Bitcoin mining. Venezuelans are using Bitcoins to purchase food from on-line merchants outside the country without going through the usual customs process that will take months. This is a good example on how people can use cryptocurrency for survival.

Security and Control

Without a single entity controlling all transactions, and instead allowing people to be in control of their own transactions, the system used in cryptocurrencies become inherently safe. Online merchants will not be able to charge add-on fees without prior notice to the customer.

Meanwhile, payments in cryptocurrencies could be made and verified without providing personal information to the transaction. Because of the fact that personal details are kept concealed, identity theft can be averted.

Security is a major feature that makes cryptocurrencies attractive to consumers. If you choose to pay using a credit card, you have to provide your personal information before you can purchase something online.

Likewise, if you need to send money through a wire, you also have to provide all the information that could also be used by frauds to pretend to be you and send money to anyone. Exchange of personal information is absent in dealing with cryptocurrencies, which increases security.

Transparency

The unique feature of cryptocurrencies such as Bitcoin is that it is anonymous yet transparent. Through the public ledger, all completed transactions can be accessed by anyone, yet personal details are concealed. The user's public address is visible for everyone but personal details are not included.

Cryptocurrencies work with great levels of transparency. All transactions involving a digital currency are publicly accessible, highly traceable, and stored permanently in the ledger. Public addresses are the only details used to define the allocations of bitcoins and where they are sent.

These addresses are privately created through individual digital wallets. But when addresses are already used, they are marked with all the records of all transactions they are involved with. Anyone in the network could access the balance as well as transactions of any user.

Because users often have to reveal their personal details before getting services or goods, the addresses used in cryptocurrencies cannot be completely anonymous. Remember, the public ledger is permanent, so all transactions can be traced. Hence, public addresses are often used once, and users are always cautious not to reveal their addresses.

One beneficiary of the transparency offered by cryptocurrencies is in the area of charity. Digital currencies are seen now as the solution for more transparency among charitable organizations, specifically on how they are spending donations.

Because of the transparent mechanism of digital currencies, every transaction is unique and can be traced. Hence, it can be easy for donors to see precisely how the organization is spending their money. There are even proposals about creating a social currency that can be used only for projects for charitable causes.

Experts also hail the advantages of digital currencies when it comes to donating funds overseas as it can considerably decrease the costs of currency trading when transferring money from one country to another. Charities can also tap into individuals and companies who have made a sizable fortune via these online currencies.

Affordable Fees

There are very minimal fees, and even no fees at all, in most cryptocurrency systems. For merchant transactions, both parties may agree on a specific amount of fee to expedite the process. Including a fee in the transaction will give more priority to the confirmation request so it will be processed faster.

Meanwhile, digital currency exchanges are important in

merchant transactions by trading cryptocurrency into conventional currency. In general, these services have lower fees compared to online bank transfers or through PayPal.

For instance, in Bitcoin, the transaction fee goes to the miner. Once a new block is created with a verified hash, the information for all the transaction will be included in the block and all transaction fees will be received by the miner who created the block.

The transaction fees in Bitcoin are voluntary, as you can still initiate a transaction even without adding a fee. In contrast, miners are also not required to accept the transactions and add them to the newly created block. Therefore, the transaction fee is just a small reward in the system to ensure that a certain transaction will be added to the next block.

Fewer Risks Involved for Merchant Transactions

Because of the fact that the transactions involving cryptocurrencies are mostly irreversible, and they are not linked to any personal details of the sender, merchants are safeguarded from possible losses that may arise due to fraud.

By using cryptocurrencies, online entrepreneurs can still do business in areas where fraud cases are high. This is due to the reason that it can be nearly impossible to cheat the system because of public record keeping and transparency.

Disadvantages of Cryptocurrencies

After exploring the basic advantages, let us now discuss the disadvantages of using cryptocurrencies:

Not Yet Widely Popular

Only very few people know the existence of cryptocurrencies, and not all of them are embracing its uses. Hence, it is a bit difficult to look for merchants who are accepting Bitcoins as payment for goods and services.

More and more businesses are accepting digital currencies because of their advantages, but the number is still a thin slice compared to businesses who prefer accepting cash or payment through credit cards.

There is still a need for people to be educated about cryptocurrencies and how they can use it in everyday living. In businesses that are accepting digital currencies, not all staff are knowledgeable enough of how these new currencies work, so there is also limit on how they can help their customers understand this area.

Workers should be educated on digital currency so that they could help their customers. This will, of course, require investment on the part of the business, but it will position the organization towards the potential commodity of the future.

Volatility

Digital currencies are volatile primarily because of the fact that there is still a limit on a number of currencies in circulation while the demand increases every day. But it is projected by experts that the volatility will decrease as time passes by. The price of digital currencies is expected to settle down as more businesses start accepting digital currencies, mainly Bitcoin.

In the traditional markets, volatility is measured by the Volatility Index. In digital currencies, volatility is not yet widely accepted since they are still in early stages. But it is a fact that Bitcoin is volatile in price compared to the US dollar.

At the moment, the price of digital currencies is influenced by the events related to this field. For example, the rate of adoption can be influenced by bad news, which includes the possible regulation by governments. Other significant new includes the controversial use of digital currencies in the drug trade in Silk Road as well as the bankruptcy of Mt. Gox in 2014.

The ensuing public panic caused the value of digital currencies to fall down rapidly versus the value of fiat currencies. In general, volatility is seen by experts as an indication that the market is progressing.

A reason why digital currencies fluctuate against conventional currencies is the conceived of value in comparison to fiat currency. Some properties of digital currencies such as Bitcoin are similar to gold.

For example, the amount of Bitcoin is fixed at 21 million BTC. Some people may choose to invest in digital currencies instead of fiat currencies since the latter is governed by governments who like to keep inflation at low, create more jobs and pose strong growth through capital resources investment.

The volatility of digital currencies is also influenced significantly by different perceptions of its intrinsic value as the method of value transfer and as a store of value. A method of value transfer refers to concept or object used to transfer property in the asset from one party to another. On the other hand, a store of value refers to the purpose of an asset to be used in the future.

The property could be saved and traded if the user deems necessary. The current volatility of digital currencies makes it an unlikely store of value. However, it offers easy transfer of value. Because these two factors influence the present spot price of digital currencies, their value could easily change according to news events similar to conventional currencies.

Still In Infancy Stage

Although gaining ground in the financial markets, digital currencies are still in its very early phase with developing features that are still very unstable. To ensure that the digital currency is secure and accessible, new services, tools, and features should be developed by the network and its supporters.

Digital currencies are still viable for growth before we can see its full function. Similar to any currency on its infancy stage, digital currencies are just starting out and should work out some areas of concern before it becomes widely accepted.

At this point, we now have explored the advantages and disadvantages of digital currencies. As you can see, cryptocurrencies, regardless of their breakthrough benefits in comparison with fiat currencies, are still not perfect. They have numerous benefits that conventional currencies cannot and may not even provide.

This is mostly because of the fact that they are still quite young and considered as a new currency. People are just starting to become aware and understand digital currencies. For its success, people should widely use them in their daily transactions.

5 - ADVANTAGES AND DISADVANTAGES OF USING CRYPTOCURRENCIES

There are always two sides of the coin. In order to understand and decide whether you want to use digital currencies or not, it is crucial to weigh both sides before you make your choice. Cryptocurrencies are breakthrough innovation, and it can be beneficial if you understand how it works and takes advantage of the early opportunity for investments and trading.

6 - Top Cryptocurrencies Aside from Bitcoin

The concept of cryptocurrencies has inspired many individuals and organizations to create their own form of digital currencies. Bitcoin is arguably the most popular digital currency today, but as of July 2016, there are more than 710 cryptocurrencies available in the market for trade and investment. However, only a few became successful to achieve $ 10 million market capitalization.

In this Chapter, we will explore the top cryptocurrencies available today. There is a separate chapter that explores Bitcoin, so we will cover here other digital currencies.

Ethereum (ETH)

Basically, Ethereum is an open platform that uses Blockchain technology, which enables developers to generate and use computer programs. Similar to Bitcoin, Ethereum is also a distributed public Blockchain network.

Even though there are some major technical differences between these two platforms, the most significant feature is that these two cryptocurrencies are substantially different when it comes to capacity and purpose.

Bitcoin provides one specific application of Blockchain technology - a P2P digital currency system, which enables online payments. While the Blockchain used in Bitcoin is used to monitor ownership of online cash, the Blockchain used in Ethereum is used to run codes of any decentralized app.

In Bitcoin, you have to mine to earn coins. In Ethereum, you have to work in order to earn Ether, which is a form of cryptocurrency, which fuels the system. Currently, Ether is a tradable cryptocurrency and can be used by app developers to pay for fees and services within the network.

Like most digital currencies, Ethereum is based on a P2P network, which any programmer can use to run Dapps or distributed applications. The network can run any computer program, but the network is designed to perform rules, which are executed if specific conditions are present similar to a contract. The Ethereum network uses its own public ledger to store, run, and secure these contracts.

Every computer on the network installs a small virtual machine that will sync with the Blockchain and remains accessible to enforce contracts. The computer network easily provides the reliability, computing capacity, and security needed to perform the stipulated arrangements.

Using the network is not free, so users only use it for consensus results and if the data are public. You can search the Ethereum Blockchain by visiting the link below:

https://www.etherchain.org/

Even though many examples of these contracts describe different human interactions, the platform is presently used for industrial use-scenarios such as communication between machines or stringent business logic between organizations.

For example, there are power companies that are looking for ways to generate a smarter grid where residences can easily buy power. Another good example is the collaboration between Samsung and IBM for Internet of Things.

Centralized networks are naturally vulnerable because they have one governing platform that could be exposed to an attack. The vision of Ethereum is to decentralize the World Wide Web by building a platform where apps could be created and run on a decentralized hub.

This prevents a single point attack, and if one area is under attack, the rest of the platform is still functional. Therefore, Ethereum is also regarded as the computer of the world, because it has the capacity for decentralizing worldwide networks and so wields unlimited power.

Prior to the development of Ethereum, Blockchain apps were created to perform very specific operations, which is quite problematic for developers. They may choose to either stretch the set of functions provided by Bitcoin or any other form of app (that is time-consuming and could be extremely difficult) or create a new Blockchain app as well as a completely new platform.

Instead of building a completely new Blockchain for every application, Ethereum allows the development of any application within the network. This really makes the Ethereum stand out from the rest of the Blockchains. It also offers the uniterceptable nature of digital currencies such as Bitcoin and stretches it to almost any app that you could think of.

This is the main reason why many experts in cryptocurrency believe that Ethereum will surpass Bitcoin as the top Blockchain, and so believed to be a hot commodity for traders and speculators.

Ethereum is planned at different stages. At present, the Ethereum project is on its second stage known as the Homestead. The four planned stages of Ethereum growth are the following:

Frontier

This stage was the initial introduction of Ethereum in 2015. This was mostly a prototype release to open the platform to more technically skilled programmers to build their own applications, initiate early mining, and start exchanges.

Homestead

Ethereum is currently on this stage. There were some changes compared to the initial plans such as the block incentive was fixed to 5 ether. In the improved Homestead, the platform becomes more of a patchwork of corrections to get rid of the risk warning that you can see on the homepage of Ethereum.

Metropolis

In this stage, the platform will be opened to the public, and the interfaces are fully tested for non-technical participants. Even though this is now being performed by individuals using the Ethereum desktop wallet. There is no definite date for this release and whether it will depend on the pace of the community.

Serenity

This is the last stage of Ethereum project and it highlights one main principle – to transform the Ethereum network from proof-of-work platform to a proof-of-stake platform, which will significantly decrease the power consumption of the Ethereum network. There is no set date for the release although experts believe this will happen in 2018.

Although the Ethereum price has already significantly risen in 2017, there is still potential to see a huge increase to as much as 100 times the present levels.

The financial world also takes a lot of advantage in using a controllable ledger, but it is a bit dubious of its privacy features. Hence, companies have made some innovation to offer Ethereum with their services to aid banks to create their own private networks.

The Ethereum network uses smart contracts, which is a phrased used to describe the code that executes the trade of money, property, content, share, or anything valuable.

When performed on the Blockchain, a smart contract will behave like an automated computer program that immediately runs the code if certain conditions are present. Because smart contracts are running on the Blockchain, they are exactly running as designed without any form of downtime, censorship, interference, or fraud.

In essence, Blockchains are designed to process code, which is mostly limited. This is not the case with Ethereum. Instead of providing a set of restricted operations, developers are free to create any operation they want inside the Ethereum network. Therefore, you can create various applications that are designed to meet specific needs.

Prior to Ethereum, the applications in Blockchains were programmed to perform a very limited set of operations.

For instance, Bitcoin was designed specifically for P2P cash transactions. Many developers experienced problems with this setup.

They may either stretch the set of functions provided by Bitcoin and other forms of applications, which is time-consuming and can be very complicated or design a new application in the Blockchain as well as a completely new platform. With this challenge, the creator of Ethereum, Vitalik Buterin, created a new platform.

The Ethereum Virtual Machine or EVM is a core innovation of the platform. It is a Turing complete software, which runs on the network and enables anyone to run any application regardless of the language used as long as there is enough memory and time in the network.

The EVM facilitates easier and more efficient processing of creating applications in the Blockchain. Rather than creating a completely new Blockchain for every new application, Ethereum allows the creation of various applications in a single platform.

Through Ethereum, developers can create and use decentralized applications with specific functions. For instance, Bitcoin is a program that allows users to transfer digital cash from one user to another. As decentralized applications are built on codes that are running the Blockchain platform, these are not subject to any central authority.

Any centralized service could be converted into a centralized platform through Ethereum. Just consider all the intermediary services that now exist across different areas including banking services, voting systems, title registries, regulatory licensing systems, and much more.

Ethereum is also currently used to create Decentralized Autonomous Organizations or DAO, which are completely decentralized and autonomous organization with no single leading entity. DAOs are running through codes, on a group of smart contracts designed inside the Blockchain used by Ethereum.

The code is written as an alternative to the structure and rules of a conventional organization, which discards the need for people and centralized control. Everyone can own a DAO by purchasing Ethereum tokens. But rather of each token being equivalent to shares and ownership, these tokens serve as contributions that provide people rights to vote.

Since decentralized applications are running on a Blockchain inside Ethereum, they can also take advantage of its properties such as zero downtime, security, risk-free, and immutability. But like other forms of Blockchains and cryptocurrencies, Ethereum and Ether also have their flaws. Although automated and digital in nature, smart contracts are still designed by humans.

Hence, these contracts are only as good as the people who designed them. Oversights and code bugs could also result in unexpected adverse effects. If there is an error in the code, the platform might be exploited, and there are very few ways to stop an attack, which involves getting the consensus of the whole network users and re-programming the core code.

The primary goal of the Ethereum network is to decentralize the World Wide Web. And arguably, it has now achieved some success of becoming the new internet platform. Ethereum has a lot of potential to become an alternative platform for hosting and executing code online.

At present, the market cap of Ethereum is around $ 17 Billion, while the market capitalization of Bitcoin is at $ 34 Billion. Hence, Ether is regarded as the second most valuable digital currency today. This number is projected to rise in a span of a few more years.

Litecoin (LTC)

Introduced in 2011, Litecoin is another type of cryptocurrency that is also based on the Bitcoin platform. This digital currency is created by Charlie Lee, a former engineer at Google and graduate of MIT.

Lee created this cryptocurrency as an open source payment platform that is also free from any interference or governance of a single authority. However, Litecoin is different from Bitcoin in areas such as using scrypt as a proof of work system and it offers faster block generation.

Litecoin was designed as a lower scale currency of Bitcoin. If Bitcoin is gold, then Litecoin is silver. It was created with the objective to improve the shortcomings of the Bitcoin network, and it has already gained support in various industries. Through the years, this digital currency has achieved liquidity and trade volume.

Litecoin production is faster than Bitcoin, specifically four times faster. In general, Litecoin is now one of the top cryptocurrencies in terms of value, but they are easier to obtain compared to most digital currencies.

Similar to other digital currencies, Litecoin also serves as an online cash system. Similar to a bank's online network or PayPal, users could use the network to transfer one currency to another. But rather than US dollars, it performs the transactions in Litecoin units. This is where the similarity of Litecoin ends.

Likewise, Litecoin is also not issued by a government. Rather than being governed by a Federal Reserve and being printed by the government, Litecoins are produced through mining as well similar to Bitcoin mining. Litecoin supply is also fixed currently at 84 million. The Litecoin network creates a block every 2.5 minutes, which is faster compared to the 10 minutes for Bitcoin.

The Litecoin block also refers to the ledger record of recent Litecoin transactions. The block is also confirmed using mining software and made accessible to any user who likes to see the block. When the miner confirms the transaction, the next block will be added to the chain.

The first user to confirm the block will receive 50 Litecoins, which is valued around $ 100. The amount of Litecoins awarded for this task decreases over time. This decreasing rate will continue at regular intervals until all miners confirmed all the 84 million Litecoins.

Mining digital currencies at a rate that is profitable for you requires super processing power, which could be done only if you have specialized software and hardware.

To mine digital currencies, the computational power of your desktop PC is not fast enough for currency mining. This brings us to another benefit of mining Litecoin as it can be mined using regular PCs. You can also mine well if your tools are high-grade.

You should take note that any currency, even the strongest ones, is only worthy if the society deems it valuable. If the Federal Reserve begins circulating too many dollars, its value will decrease. Anything that becomes cheaply available becomes less valuable.

The developers of Litecoin are well aware of this from the very start and they understood that it can be difficult for a new digital currency to gain a reputation in the growing marketplace. But by limiting the number of Litecoins that are in circulation, the developers can at least minimize the fears of people on overproduction.

As we have already mentioned, Litecoin is modeled after the Bitcoin network. Hence, the way to get Litecoins is, to begin with, a Bitcoin account, then trade BTCs for LTCs. The current exchange rate of BTC to LTC is 146 to 1. You might be thinking about the possible benefit of trading a cryptocurrency to a less popular one.

There are several advantages that are inherent to Litecoin, which makes it attractive to use the newer digital currency. Primarily, Litecoin can process more transactions, mainly because of the shorter time for generating a block.

Litecoin also has a lot cheaper transaction fee, posted at 1/1000 of a Litecoin no matter what the volume of the transaction. At the current exchange rate, this is only about

2 cents, which is a lot cheaper compared to the 3% fee on PayPal.

In the actual world, the most dependable stores of value are the currencies of choice during a crisis. For example, Zimbabwe faced hyperinflation starting in the 1990s that wiped out the fortunes of many people.

The currency became the least valuable currency in the world in which Z$ Trillion was only equivalent to 40 cents in US dollars. People had to use more stable currencies such as US dollars, Chinese Yuan, Japanese Yen, and South African Rand for their everyday purchases. The inherent scarcity of Litecoin prevents hyperinflation. The main challenge at the present is to gain widespread use.

When a currency achieves a significant volume of users who agree that the currency is valuable, it will result in stability and sustainability. Litecoin is not yet widely accepted, as there are only fewer than 100,000 current users today. However, as digital currencies become more widely accepted and their values become stable, they will become the currencies of the future.

Ripple (XRP)

Introduced in 2012, Ripple is a real-time worldwide settlement network, which provides affordable overseas payments. This digital currency allows banks to complete international payments in real-time at a fraction of a cost and transparency. With a market capitalization around $ 1.26 billion, Ripple is one of the most valuable digital currencies today.

Similar to Bitcoin and Litecoin, Ripple also maintains a Blockchain known as a consensus ledger as its method of confirmation. However, it does not require mining so it decreases the need to use the computational power and also lessen network latency.

The developers of Ripple believes that value distribution is a great way to incentivize specific behaviors and so they are now distributing the currency mainly via business development deals, offering XRP to organizational buyers who are interested to invest in the currency, and as rewards to providers of liquidity who provide tighter payment spreads.

Even though it was only introduced in 2012, Ripple is actually older than Bitcoin. The project was actually implemented in 2004 by Ryan Fugger who envisioned it as a decentralized monetary system that can effectively empower individuals and organizations in generating their own money.

Basically, Ripple is represented as debt. The transactions are simply composed of balances being transformed on a series of digital cash reserves from one user to another. Let us consider a simple example to explain how Ripple works in practice.

Let us say that there are two friends, Beatrice and Claire who starts road journey. They have decided to bring their own friends. Beatrice brought her cousin Amanda, while Claire invited her friend Donna. Amanda knows Beatrice, but has never met Claire and Donna before. Likewise, Donna has never met Amanda and Beatrice. Let's say that Amanda and Donna want to buy coffee, but Donna doesn't have cash.

So Amanda pays for her coffee at $2 per cup, and Donna promises to pay Amanda back using Ripple. Because it makes no sense to have Donna owe $2 to Amanda, as she may well never have the chance to pay back, she instead agrees to owe $2 to Claire. Claire agrees to owe $2 to Beatrice and Beatrice agrees to owe $2 to Amanda.

Let us assume that Beatrice has an outstanding debt of $1 to Claire prior to the meeting. In this scenario, the debt will be canceled and Claire now only has $1 debt to Beatrice. The main point here is that all debts are between people who have chosen to establish a trust relationship or in financial jargon a credit line.

Hence, they trust each other that they will pay the debt when one party requires money. Through this system, cash could revolve around even between people who don't know each other.

In some areas, this system is actually similar to the way our banking system already works today. Overseas money transfers are collected by banks, cash transfers between banks are canceled out, and then when a bank releases more money compared to what it takes, the banks will replenish cash through different systems designed for this purpose.

The original Ripple project aims to achieve a democratization of this system, so anyone can serve as a bank - capable of receiving and serving as a channel for loans.

The original Ripple project achieves some level of success, and the system can still be accessed on villages.cc and classic.ripplpay.com. But these communities who are using the classic Ripple were far from becoming universal as they never extended beyond the small communities.

This is mainly due to the simple reason that before anyone can join the network, he or she should already have a friend within the network. Or else, there is no way to build a chain of cash reserves between you and other users, so completing a transaction can be impossible.

Another flaw is the centralized software. Even though Fugger aims to create a cash system that was distributed and anyone can participate, the network that monitors all the cash lines and balances must still be controlled in a central hub.

Today, the Ripple network has been improved. The issue in isolated communities is now addressed in two ways: a gateway system and a specialized Ripple currency. The latter is not debt-based unlike other things stored in the network. Hence, the currency could be sent from one user to another just like other digital currencies.

It is now possible to send money to someone who is not part of your local trust network. You just need to convert the currency into XRP, send over the network, which will convert it back. Ripple's built-in decentralized exchange hub converts the currency, so there is now way for users to back off from the deal, as the transaction is recorded into the ledger simultaneously.

Another significant development in the improved Ripple system are the integration of gateways, which are basically a commercial service that serves the role of being a credit middle channel for those who are not yet in the network or possibly those who are not yet connected through someone they know in the network and prefers to use the commercial service.

The gateway will serve as the first layer of the link in the trust chain between the user and the recipient when the user likes to complete a payment, as well as the last link when the user likes to receive money. You can trust several gateways simultaneously, so the network will still maintain a decentralized approach, which is comparable to mining hubs.

Anyone can become a gateway in the Ripple network, which provides a long continuum of network topologies that range from a model of a centralized banking system to a P2P cash system.

During the initial stages, the creators of Ripple believe that gateways will emerge as the norm. But with the growth and success of Ripple, it could happen that as the system gets enough market share, a peer to peer system will eventually rise.

Like in other digital currency platforms, the Ripple gateways are not completely unflawed. Primarily, there is no inherent system to make certain that the gateways will not default on its debts. Also, those who have been using digital currencies such as Bitcoin and Litecoin, are not completely convinced of using a network that needs trust in third-party organizations for its functions.

At this point, Ripple developers are still not offering solutions for these concerns. The Ripple network does not offer a solid solution to this problem, and controlling fraudulent gateways should be done by more conventional mechanisms.

Decentralization is the other primary aspect of Ripple. In essence, the mechanism of Ripple is to monitor the balances, which is pretty much the same as Bitcoin. The Blockchain used by Ripple also uses public and private keys, addresses, and changes to the database are also performed via a system of digitally signed transactions.

As a matter of fact, Ripple uses exactly the same specifications as Bitcoins aside from the primary byte in the address format. Hence, anyone can use the same keys to verify transactions and messages in the Ripple and Bitcoin networks. But instead of mining, the transactions in Ripple are basically propagated via the network, and a given set of contradictory transactions.

For instance, let's say that a fraudulent user initiating transactions to send the same $50 to five various merchants with the hope of receiving $250 worth of goods. The clients should verify first which one received the payment first, and if unverified will be marked as illegitimate, via a process called consensus.

In general, Consensus is an improved platform that is already being used in Bitcoin network for transactions requiring no confirmations. Private nodes decide what version of a new ledger should be accepted through a poll to see the opinion of the majority, which allows the system to easily settle on one choice only.

This process is a bit faster compared to the block confirmation in Bitcoin where a new ledger state is generated about five to 10 seconds, which allow for nearly automatic verification.

Other digital currencies that you might be interested to learn about are Dash, Manero, Altcoins, and much more.

7 - How to Make Money in Crypto-currency

There are strong indications that digital currencies will become widely accepted in the near future. And similar to fiat currencies that most of us use today, you can harness the benefits of cryptocurrencies in order to make money.

In this Chapter, we will discuss the recommended methods that you can try to make money in specific cryptocurrencies.

Bitcoin Mining

We have already discussed how Bitcoin mining works earlier in this book, so in this section, we will provide you the technical and strategic details on how you can make money through mining Bitcoins.

Basically, Bitcoin miners are not people, because the actual mining is performed by a hardware, essentially a supercomputer used to execute the sophisticated mathematical computations needed to encrypt and decrypt processes on the network.

For the sake of discussion, we will refer to this hardware as miners or Bitcoin miners, while those who are running the hardware will be called ledger managers or Bitcoin ledger managers.

After mining for Bitcoins for some time, you will learn that this activity is highly technical, so in the part of a ledger manager, it can be an easy task because you really don't need to do anything. However, it really involves sophisticated algorithms and tons of math.

But it is not necessary to master these computations before you can make money from mining. Rather, we will only discuss the important things for you to begin with Bitcoin mining and determine if you can really make some profit.

Bitcoin was developed to prevent any type of centralized regulation, similar to governments and banks have over fiat currencies. This is what makes the cryptocurrency unique, and this is also what provides Bitcoin its advantage as a currency.

In order for the Bitcoin system to work, without outside interference, miners play an important role in maintaining the Blockchain and monitor all transactions on the network.

Every time a transaction happens, all miners verify their ledgers and adjust the chain accordingly.

Bitcoin mining is actually a numbers game, where everyone has a number, each transaction has a number, and every Bitcoin has a number. As a matter of fact, it is more accurate to say that everything in a Bitcoin is a number instead of has a number.

Every time that there is a transaction, the system will generate a number, and Bitcoin miners will work to confirm the transaction by decoding the encryption.

How to Get Started in Bitcoin Mining

Before you can make money in Bitcoin mining, you should first invest in the recommended hardware. And just a heads up, it can be expensive. You might need to spend a few thousand dollars if you want to keep up with the growing user base and demand in the Bitcoin network.

For example, one suggested hardware is the ASIC Bitcoin miner Antminer S7 28nm, which costs around $ 2,600. But there are still miners that only cost for as low as $400.

During the early years of Bitcoin, ledger managers began with regular PCs that are only used for Bitcoin mining. With the rise of Bitcoin as a digital currency, mining called for higher computational power. For as short as one year, ledger managers used PCs installed with a special card designed solely for Bitcoin mining. Since then, more sophisticated Bitcoin miners have been introduced.

It is important to take note that being a ledger manager requires continuous investment as with the projected widespread use of Bitcoin, more and more ledger managers will participate in the network, and as a result, better ways will be eventually developed.

On average, new Bitcoin miners are developed at least once a year, but there is no guarantee. Apart from the Bitcoin miner, you also have to use a specific power supply, which may range from $ 60 to $ 800, and even more depending on the requirements by the miner.

Aside from the cost of the mining tools, you also need to consider the power cost. Bitcoin miners consume some electricity, so you have to factor in this cost. For instance, if you are paying around 20 cents for every kilowatt, one Bitcoin miner may cost you about $ 6 every day.

But if you are running the right hardware, and you are living in an area where power is affordable, then you only need to consider a few dollars each day.

The cost of power for every kilowatt is varying from one state to another. So far, the east coast has the highest cost, with as high as 15 cents per kilowatt in Florida. Be sure to consider this as it can be useless to go for Bitcoin mining if the cost is higher than what you can earn. But how much money can you make in Bitcoin mining?

The Bitcoin network is designed to integrate blocks of transactions for every 10 minutes. Hence, you can't decrypt every transaction as they are made. Your hardware has to perform this in blocks.

Every block is worth around 25 BTCs. However, the price of the actual coin will depend on the present conversion rate of Bitcoin, which will vary from day to day. As of this writing, 1 BTC is equivalent to $ 2,749.94. Hence, for every block, you can solve or verify, you can earn a total of $ 68,748.50.

There are two methods you can try to earn money through

Bitcoin mining: solo mining and pool mining.

As the name suggests, solo mining refers to the lone strategy of mining on your own. You set up all the needed hardware. Then you play the race of decrypting a block before other miners succeed.

The second method is known as pool mining, in which you participate in a group of ledger managers who are coordinating with each other for decoding the blocks. For every block that your group solves, you share in the payment, depending on how much work your hardware allocated.

You might need around $ 3,000 to $ 5,000 to get started in Bitcoin Mining. Many ledger managers are using several miners to increase their odds of solving the blocks first.

Other Ways of Making Money in Bitcoin

Mining is not the only way to make money in the Bitcoin market. You could also try speculation trading in the stock markets or by trading Bitcoins. In 2010, the cost of Bitcoin was only $12 per coin.

Seven years later, its price skyrocketed to $2,749.94. You

could have been a millionaire if you purchased $ 5,000 worth of Bitcoins in 2010. But of course, there is always the risk of volatility, as trading Bitcoin has the same inherent risk in the stock market.

It takes time to learn how you can invest in stocks through Bitcoin. There are several ETF, which trades on Bitcoin depending on the movement of the price. This has similar mechanism in investing in gold ETF.

One company may purchase the commodity or invests in companies that depend on this commodity then sell the share of the company. You actually don't have ownership of the coins, but your stocks move alongside the commodity price.

Becoming an exchanger is possibly the easiest way to make a profit through Bitcoin trading. You just need to sign up with a P2P exchange marketplace such as LocalBitcoins or BitSquare, then you can start offering an exchange service in a local area for buying and selling Bitcoins.

Adding a spread will allow you to make some profit. For instance, a buy offer for 2 per cent below market price and sell offer for 2 per cent above the selling price. People are usually happy with this spread if you can provide easy ways for anyone to trade Bitcoins.

However, you should be aware that you might probably need to secure some deals first by responding to other people's ads and then shouldering the cost of the initial spread so you can start getting a good reputation in the industry

You don't really need to become a master in financial analysis before you can become a Bitcoin exchanger. This is the reason why it is easy for this to start. Becoming a digital currency trader requires more skill and knowledge. As a trader, you may need to use online exchanges and you can purchase or sell depending on whether the people will believe the price will fall or rise.

You can also provide a service of filling up order books, which could be taken up by individuals who want to trade for more practical reasons. However, your focus may not be on offering a service to customers, providing great customer service, or nurturing relationships. Your focus could simply on getting offers as a form of guessing game if the market will rise or fall.

If you are interested to become a Bitcoin trader, providing P2P exchange service could be an ideal way to begin. As long as the market doesn't fluctuate that much, it can be possible for the trader to make more profit regardless of the price movement.

But simultaneously, if the market follows an upward trend, then it is recommended to purchase more. Hence, a Bitcoin exchanger can also make more profit by becoming a Bitcoin trader while providing exchange services for those who are not yet decided to become a trader to minimize the risk and also to test the waters.

Even with exchanges done on a centralized hub, where you don't usually deal with your customers, you can still make profits by providing exchange services. You can do this by creating instead of taking offers. When you place offers into the orderbooks instead of accepting offers that are already there, you can possibly gain a better price.

Since you are also offering a service, you also serve the role of being the market maker who enables the exchange center to serve as an exchanger even without the large capital. Most exchanges will also provide you some rewards to motivate you to become a maker instead of being a taker. This could come in the form of decreased trading fees, zero trading fees, or even rewards and bonuses.

Top Strategies for Bitcoin Trading

A well-defined and clear strategy will increase your chances of success in Bitcoin trading. You have to know precisely what you like when you are opening a trade, how much profit you like prior to building up before you can take the offer, your loss tolerance, and much more. You have to clearly identify what timescale you are looking at and what forms of changes will make you rethink your strategy.

Monitoring the Trend

Financial markets usually have long-term price trends, in which the general movement follows a single direction for months and even years. There are some minor fluctuations, but in general, the trend will remain clear.

Some traders in digital currencies will just look for this long-term trend and trade in this direction. There is even no need to identify the point at which a trend would turn and a new one starts in the opposing direction, as long as you don't need to make a withdrawal anytime soon.

When an average trend requires around a year to complete, then it is really pointless if it may take you six months to be sure that it is a new trend.

Technical Analysis

Technical Analysis involves the use of chart patterns and mathematical formulae to project the future direction of price movement. This analysis is completely based on the past price data and possibly volume data. Hence, it says nothing about if the price is too low or too high objectively. Instead, you have to determine if there are particular recurring trends and patterns that will soon appear on the market.

Most of these are heavily postulated on human psychology – the notion that people just need to act in a specific way to different movement in prices. Some traders also believe that changes in the real underlying value are already priced by participants in the market, and so taking a closer look at the actions of the people in the market can provide you a hint and guide your decision for trading.

Fundamental Analysis

If you are into the stock market, you will surely be familiar with fundamental analysis, which you can also use as a recommended strategy for trading bitcoins.

In this strategy, you have to look at the fundamental information that may affect the price of a digital currency such as a number of coins traded on exchange centers, number of active digital wallets versus the number of digital wallets, number of cryptocurrency transactions every day, and much more.

You can then use this data to project what you believe Bitcoin will be worth at the moment, then decide if you think it is presently overvalued or undervalued, and then trade according to your assessment.

News Watch

Market price will usually rise or fall depending on what is on the news. For instance, the news of Bitcoin website being hacked or an announcement from the government that it will start regulating cryptocurrencies might result to a price down, while new funding for new startups or large companies accepting cryptocurrencies will cause the price to rise.

Trading cryptocurrencies based on news alone is not an ideal strategy, as it can be difficult to always read the news first and respond accordingly.

More often than not, the market might already have made some movement before you can even act – even though if you have the time to always read the news or you have set up an app to send you instant notifications on relevant news, then you might be able to get there first.

Another approach is to leverage on corrections. Usually, the market over reacts to significant news stories as people could jump on or get caught in the moment, without really thinking through it. For example, a 15% fall is usually immediately followed by a 5% increase as the market may rectify this over reaction. This is another opportunity for you to leverage the news and make some profit.

Swing Trade

The methods described above are strategies for the medium or long term. You may need to wait several months or years before you can build a good return for your efforts, and there is always the possibility to end up making small profits or take losses for many months.

Day trading is a faster-paced approach to make money. This strategy refers to the buying and selling Bitcoins based on the short-term movements in the price, usually over the course of hours or days instead of months or years.

Swing Trading is the most common strategy for day trading. This approach utilized a range of technical indicators to search for the turning points in trends at short-term. You can make a profit from the daily swings depending on the fluctuations of the price of the digital currency regardless of whether the long-term movement is rising or falling.

This usually involves searching for resistance and support levels. A resistance level refers to the rising price movement where traders are expected to resist the sellers taking a profit, while a support level refers to the falling price level where buyers are expected to resist into the market to gain from an expected bargain.

Take note that the Bitcoin market has high volatility, which means each part of it relies on something else that makes it quite impossible to know what to do when it comes to making a profit.

Factor in the added work of setting up the hardware, as well as solving maintenance needs, it can be said that Bitcoin mining requires passion and enthusiasm. You need money to make money so you have to invest in the recommended hardware. In addition, you might be at a significant disadvantage if you are not that technically savvy. Also, don't expect a stable income from Bitcoin mining.

Arguably, Bitcoin mining is not the best way to make money online, considering the sheer number of challenges you have to overcome. But this is the reason why the rewards are hefty, as not everyone can do it.

How to Make Money with Ethereum

At its current phase, Ethereum is just similar Bitcoin when it was first released in 2009. There was even this story about a man purchasing Bitcoins worth $27 in 2009, but then forgot about it. Year after he discovered that the value ballooned to $ 980,000. Hence, people are excited about Ethereum as it is poised to become the next Bitcoin or even surpass the digital currency.

There are great indicators suggesting that buying Ethereum is good for long-term investments.

Primarily, the technology used in building the Ethereum network can be used for several purposes. Hence, it is a breakthrough technology with the capacity to affect many industries. In addition, the value of Ethereum as a digital currency will continue to rise as the demand for the plat-form and its smart contracts continue to rise.

When it comes to stability, Ethereum shows an organic growth without large spikes, and it indicates predictability and stability. The rising value and demand of a specific cryptocurrency are a good sign of its potential. Regardless of the reason, it still increases the demand, which will affect the current price of Ethereum.

Ethereum also starts to create waves in the established industry. Teams from MIT are now conducting active research on Ethereum, while IBM and Microsoft are also offering Ethereum as a Blockchain service. The design of Ethereum as a world computer has enticed significant individuals such as Bill Gates.

Where and How to Buy Ethereum?

There are different platforms online where you can buy Ethereum such as Coinbase, which serves like a digital wallet. This is available to users in more than 30 countries such as United States, Canada, Singapore, United Kingdom, Belgium, Croatia, Denmark, France, Hungary, Italy, Malta, Norway, Netherlands, Poland, Spain, Switzerland, Sweden, and more.

Today, Coinbase is the largest broker of digital currencies where you can purchase Ethereum and Bitcoin with a linked bank account, Interac Online, SEPA transfer, and other common payment methods.

The Coinbase dashboard is quite user-friendly, and easy for new users to trade Ethereum and Bitcoin. Moreover, it is easy to purchase cryptocurrencies using your debit card or credit card.

Coinbase headquarters is located in San Francisco and funded by the biggest investors in fintech today, so it is pretty much a reliable platform.

The first step that you have to do is to register for a Coinbase account, which will provide you a secure place to keep your Ethereum as well as easy payment methods to transform your local currency into Bitcoin or Ethereum. Currently, when you register for a Coinbase account, you can get free $10 worth of Bitcoin if you trade $ 100 worth of Bitcoins.

The next step is to link your accounts such as debit card, credit card, or bank account. You also have to finish some confirmation steps prior to using your Coinbase account. When you complete the verification steps, you can now start trading Ethereum or Bitcoin.

After initiating your first purchase, the network will fulfill your order and deliver your purchased currencies. Take note that the price of Ether changes every day, so the dashboard will show you the prevailing exchange rate before you purchase.

At present, Ether is priced high in the market, and there is still the possibility to increase up to 100 times its current value.

Ethereum Mining

Mining for Bitcoin began with basic bare and bones GPU and CPU mining, which could be performed on high-powered PCs prior to the development of ASIC miners that caused the introduction of specialized hardware. However, the Blockchain used by Ethereum is a lot more resistant to these miners, which has expedited the processing even with using only GPUs.

If you are using a high-powered gaming system, then you already have a hardware that is capable enough for Ether mining. While you can mine Ethereum as an individual, you can still gain better results by working in a pool.

However, you should still consider the increasing challenge associated to a price hike. Ether is at an all-time high price today, but it can be pointless to mine if power costs are now so high. Moreover, the developers of Ethereum have arguably a neutral view when it comes to mining.

As a result, about 90 per cent of all miners for the Bitcoin Blockchain are from China, which causes considerable political strife as well as a lack of innovation. The developers of Ethereum are well aware of this and so they are trying to come up with a solution.

At this point, it may not be the best idea to invest heavily in equipment for mining Ethereum as it could be difficult for you to become profitable in the long-term.

8 - The Future of Cryptocurrency

We may still wait for a decade before any state government official recognizes Bitcoin or any other digital currency as a preferred currency. Just recently, Bitcoin experienced 35% price fluctuation after the US government denied the proposal of the Winklevos Bitcoin Trust for exchange trading.

The US Securities and Exchange Commissioned denied the said proposal mainly because of concerns that Bitcoin might be used for illegal purposes such as drugs trade, terrorism funding, and black market trading. But there is still hope and in the next few years, we might see some significant progress for alternative currencies we have.

While Bitcoin experienced some price drop, a more affordable cryptocurrency – Ether – has recently reached its all-time high price. Even though the current setup of Ether prevents you from using it for direct payment, digital currencies in general still seem to have a brighter future because of new innovations such as smart contracts.

Furthermore, more privacy-focused digital currency alternatives are beginning to gain popularity in favor of platforms like Bitcoin that in spite of their tight security measures, still has some loopholes that could be taken advantage for personal data.

Another exciting news is the acceptance of Bitcoin in academic organizations pioneered by the University of Ohio in their Bitcoin classes as an integral part of its MFE curriculum. Other colleges in the US are also now accepting Bitcoins, which is a significant progress in the journey of cryptocurrencies in the mainstream.

In general, this acceptance of Bitcoin has already resulted in several companies considering large investment opportunities in cryptocurrency, which further fuels its destiny to become mainstream.

It might be too early to say that digital currencies will become the norm, but now we are certain that they are gaining popularity as we progress into a new age.

Why Cryptocurrencies Are Seen As Dangerous Innovation?

Financial organizations around the world have mixed response to the existence of self-regulating cryptocurrencies that are now gradually gaining popularity. Most banks are now reviewing their business model, specifically trying to search for answers on how digital currencies will affect their business.

However, some banking experts suggest that digital currencies can, in fact, be used by banks to underscore the security of conventional banking systems versus Blockchain technologies.

We now regularly read news reports about the volatility of cryptocurrencies like Bitcoin and Ether, because of the unstable and variable trading value in the previous years.

Even though these digital currencies are on their all-time high, it is still worthy to take note that in 2013, the value of Bitcoin dramatically dropped from $200 to $60 in only a matter of three months, and then rise again to around $1250 after seven months.

In addition, the low liquidity of Bitcoin also plays an integral part in how it is being embraced in the trading industry, mainly because liquidity usually determines how many partners are open to trade with the commodity. Experts in the financial markets suggest that the low liquidity of cryptocurrencies mean they are now considered as high-risk investment.

Financial experts also suggest that even though there are few ways to minimize the risk of digital currencies at present, Bitcoin traders are usually not influenced by negative news on digital currencies.

Remember, the inherent volatility of Bitcoin is still a high risk for many investors and organizations, and as indicators suggest, there is no great way to hedge this risk. Hence, most brokers and institutions may decide to put off their investment at the moment, and this is just playing safe.

Meanwhile, there are still thousands of individuals and organizations who are investing in Bitcoins, and this suggests that they are putting their trust on the digital currency as a mainstream commodity in the future.

The World Wide Impact of Digital Currencies

Even though the United Kingdom has already announced

its openness to trading digital currencies, China is being hostile to this new cash platform.

At the peak of Bitcoin's popularity in China, its value significantly dropped because of government restrictions and hostility. In 2013, China officially banned financial organizations from trading cryptocurrencies and regulators also thwarted payment organizations from trading Bitcoins. Of course, this has caused detrimental effects on the success of Bitcoin in China.

Before the ban, China was regarded as the largest world market for Bitcoin and its prices were even higher compared to the US and European exchanges. But this all changed when the Chinese government officially opposed the use of cryptocurrencies in Chinese soil.

Even though Bitcoin is still legal in China, it can be very difficult to use because of the restrictions and hostility imposed by the government on individuals and financial organizations. Experts believe that it is a major challenge for Bitcoin in China to be accepted and the government hostility will not likely to change until this focus changes.

Basically, the challenge for digital currencies in China is focused more on mining and speculation instead of genuine acceptance. Take note that the currency's value is dependent on its acceptance and use by the society for exchanging goods or services.

Even though some businesses started to accept Bitcoins as payment in China, the Chinese society, in general, was not focused on cultivating acceptance, but instead feeding and fueling speculation.

Why are some governments like China hostile to digital currencies? Experts believe that on the point of view of a government, cryptocurrencies pose possible risks to the economy of a nation because they will allow people to complete large transactions out from the country without government interference usually in form of tax.

For instance, if regular people can easily buy overseas involving Bitcoins that is worth millions of dollars, the economy might collapse if not at least falter. Regulating the use of Bitcoin today, while still monitoring its worldwide acceptance allows the government to control the risk while still being open to the advantages of cryptocurrencies.

Most financial organizations and governments around the world are demonstrating a wait and see strategy when it comes to cryptocurrencies. There are few financial experts who believe that cryptocurrencies will be just a fad, so they may just disappear after some years, while others trust in the platform as the future of our payments.

As more and more cryptocurrencies are introduced, there is a higher opportunity for competitors to innovate more platforms that would overtake the top cryptocurrencies today. The future cryptocurrencies could change our current business and societal landscape if they can provide better stability and higher liquidity than Bitcoin.

9 - Conclusion

Thanks again for taking the time to purchase this book!

You should now have a good understanding of cryptocurrencies, and be able to guide your decision whether to use digital currencies or even harness its advantages for you to make money.

Thank You

As we reach the end of this book, I want to say thanks for reading this book.

I want to get this information out to as many people as possible. If you found this book helpful, I would greatly appreciate you leaving me a review. This helps others find the book as well.

Disclaimer

This document is geared towards providing exact and reliable information in regards to the topic and issue covered. The publication is sold on the idea that the publisher is not required to render an accounting, officially permitted, or otherwise, qualified services. If advice is necessary, legal, financial, medical or professional, a practiced individual in the profession should be ordered.

This information is not presented by a financial or medical practitioner and is for entertainment, educational and informational purposes only. The content is not intended as a substitute for professional medical advice, diagnosis, or treatment. Always seek the advice of your physician or other qualified health care provider with any questions you may have regarding a medical condition. Never disregard professional medical advice or delay in seeking it because of something you have read.

The information provided herein is stated to be truthful and consistent, in that any liability, in terms of inattention or otherwise, by any usage or abuse of any policies, processes, or directions contained within is the solitary and utter responsibility of the recipient reader. Under no circumstances